The
New Art of
Living

Books by Norman Vincent Peale

ADVENTURES IN THE HOLY LAND

THE AMAZING RESULTS OF POSITIVE THINKING

THE COMING OF THE KING

ENTHUSIASM MAKES THE DIFFERENCE

A GUIDE TO CONFIDENT LIVING

HE WAS A CHILD

THE HEALING OF SORROW

INSPIRING MESSAGES FOR DAILY LIVING

JESUS OF NAZARETH

NOT DEATH AT ALL

THE POWER OF POSITIVE THINKING

THE POWER OF POSITIVE THINKING FOR YOUNG PEOPLE

SIN, SEX, AND SELF-CONTROL

STAY ALIVE ALL YOUR LIFE

THE TOUGH-MINDED OPTIMIST

TREASURY OF COURAGE AND CONFIDENCE

YOU CAN WIN

With Dr. Smiley Blanton:

THE ART OF REAL HAPPINESS

FAITH IS THE ANSWER

NORMAN VINCENT PEALE

The New Art of Living

HAWTHORN BOOKS, INC.   NEW YORK

W. Clement Stone, Publisher

TO MY FATHER
and
TO MY MOTHER

Charles Clifford and Anna DeLaney Peale

My exemplars in
THE ART OF LIVING

A Word to the Reader

Back in 1937 I wrote my first book. Nineteen others have followed.

Always I have cherished a sort of special feeling for that first effort to communicate my ideas about effective living. It had an ambitious title: "The Art of Living." Many readers spoke graciously of it, declaring that it was of benefit to them in their own lives.

Examining the book recently it came to me that it still has a message that is pertinent to the present time even though it was published thirty-four years ago. In re-reading "The Art of Living" I became aware once again of the continuity of human problems. In this book we dealt with basic concerns such as fear, tension, guilt, defeat; and suggested workable solutions. People gained victories by following this book as a guide.

Then I reflected that in the nineteen books that followed this one, in each succeeding time period the same old problems were still and always prevalent. But the same true answers were also available—true because they are God's answers to human need in any time. Human need goes on forever, but so does God continue the same.

So the art of living today, though approached in a changed climate, still partakes of the unchangeable truth in Christ who is "the same yesterday, today and forever."

The advantage of revamping for a new era an old book which had to do with personal problems in its time is that it demonstrates anew the power of unchanging truth in a changing world.

Setting to work to update the book by removing references contemporary to the thirties, I hope and believe the present manuscript has a vital message for people of the seventies. Thus we are republishing the book under the title, *The New Art of Living*. For the principles of creative and effective living which it contains are timeless and have the same practical value as formerly. I believe *The New Art of Living* is definitely geared to your problems today and every day. May it prove of real value to you as you live in the now generation.

Norman Vincent Peale

Preface

Everyone who scans these pages is alive. The fact that he is able to sit up and run his eyes over these words is proof of that. It does not follow, however, that being alive he knows the art of living. We are, many of us, in the strange anomaly of living and yet not living. The body functions; its surpassing mechanism does its part well. We live and move and have our being in the flesh, and yet, sadly enough, many miss the joy of life. Hamlet, as all may testify, was not the last man to find his days—"stale, flat, and unprofitable." It is, when you think of it, a peculiar thing for a man to live and yet not live. There is manifestly something decidedly wrong with it. The thing does not make sense.

In a way we are all philosophers. We would rather apathetically like to know the origin and destiny of human life, but at best these are to us academic questions which, while satisfying to the inquiring spirit, more or less developed in us all, are not our chief concern. What we eagerly want to know is how to extract the most in contentment and satisfaction from these hurrying years we call our time.

Nor will we be content with theories, however finely spun. Excellent treatises on life and its infinite ramifications, however exhaustive and commendable their scholarship, do not meet the requirements of the practical question raised here. The hard-pressed man of today, surrounded as he is by the most elaborate array of problems ever to distract human intelligence, earnestly wants one question answered and in terms he can understand and appreciate. That question boldly and baldly stated is, "Tell me how to live here and now in a way that will bring me satisfaction and peace and give me sense of meaning." From the scholar to the ignoramus, from the millionaire to the pauper, from the capitalist to the communist, in varying form and style, that is the great question and desire of men everywhere. All other questions, however significant, take second place to that problem.

The author believes that the principles of Jesus Christ contain the secret of the satisfactory life. But ever-increasing masses of the people fail to attend church and so do not come under the influence of its teaching. Moreover, these people feel that the Church does not generally talk in the language and thought forms of the common man, with the result that they neither understand nor are greatly interested in giving spiritually oriented living a trial. The gospel and its power to help everyday people in their everyday lives needs to be restated in simple, current phrase. The workable technique of spiritual power needs to be retaught. The purpose of this book is to give practical help to men and women everywhere in the greatest of all arts, the art of living.

THE AUTHOR.

New York City.

Contents

The
New Art of
Living

One

MEET YOURSELF

Life begins today for the person who meets himself.
At whatever age this great event occurs, life, deep and
full, wells up and from that time on it can truly be
said one lives. Strangely enough, multitudes of men
and women are born, spend their days and die, never
having really known themselves. They come and go
on the human scene, the possessors of unrealized
powers which never quite find expression. Of such
Holmes pathetically declared, "They died with all
their music in them." Human waste of such magnitude
is little short of tragic and constitutes an offense against
creation.

Our problem is to become acquainted with our
own selves, letting our personalities loose upon the
world for the sheer adventure of their full development and in the positive hope that they may in their
own way lift the level of humanity.

Long ago Socrates wrote over the old Greek Temple
—"Know Thyself"—for he realized that achievement
in any field and in the art of living itself is dependent

11

upon an accurate knowledge of oneself. The average
man needs this injunction of the Father of Philosophy,
for most of us have no adequate conception of our
powers and abilities. At heart we underestimate ourselves. We do not really believe in ourselves and
remain for that reason weak, ineffectual, even impo-
tent, when we could be strong, dominant, victorious.

An old cobbler in Edinburgh, with that mature
wisdom not infrequently found in the simple, honorable trades, was in the habit of beginning each day
with the prayer, "O Lord, give me a high opinion of
myself." To be sure, there are some people who seem
to possess this lofty personal respect without necessity for recourse to the expedient of prayer, but it
yet remains that the mass of men do not have a high
opinion of themselves, and the reason is they do not
know themselves.

Dynamic of Self-Realization

The greatest day in any individual's life is when he
begins for the first time to realize himself. For some
this fortunately happens early in life and it bestows
upon them a decided advantage. For others it happens late, but when it does the monotony of the unresponsive years is made to shine in the reflected glory
of the late afternoon sunburst. Whether it be early or
late, any of us may well seek unremittingly the exciting experience of personal realization.

It happened to a college student friend of mine once with dramatic suddenness. Genial, easygoing, he was as unsuccessful in his studies as he was efficient upon the athletic field. His popularity with the cheering section was not fully shared by the faculty, and the curtain was slowly but surely falling upon his academic career. Its final drop, for some not too obscure reason, awaited only the conclusion of the football season.

Destiny, however, has its own strange ways. One day in a class in psychology our student friend suddenly became enthralled as the professor described how the average man fails because he does not learn to control and consolidate his powers. He used the familiar illustration of the burning glass. The rays of the sun, falling upon a piece of paper, have little effect. Let them, however, be drawn by the burning glass to a focus and they create an intense heat which will quickly burn a hole in the paper.

The professor pointed out that the man who succeeds is the one who can draw his dissipated and therefore futile powers to a focus. Our student said that in a flashing illumination he saw the cause of his own failure and oblivious of all in the room and under the spell of a veritable new birth leaped to his feet, crying, "I see it; I see it." Whereupon, amidst titters of amusement, he sank back embarrassed but wonderingly happy into his seat. What had happened? He had met himself, a new self, his real self, which never before had received its day in the sun, and the revelation changed him from a failure to a potential success, the possibilities of which were later abundantly realized.

Learn to Appreciate Yourself

A similar experience may be gained by any person who desires it strongly enough to put himself and keep himself in the way of finding it. The first step is to plant in your mind the seed of a wholesome self-appreciation. You must cultivate a genuine understanding of the worth and significance of yourself and of all men. This is made necessary by the fact that we live in a time in which we have been surfeited by a multitude of cheap ideas as to what we are.

The growing knowledge of the universe, which in the past half century revealed the vastness of the cosmos, gave rise to the notion that man is correspondingly insignificant. The new scientific control over nature caused the development of the theory that the spiritual force called God is either nonexistent or, at least, not quite so necessary to humanity as had been believed, for had not man discovered that he could use science as an Aladdin's Lamp to give him all he desired and God no longer was needed except for a few remaining superstitious, religious souls?

As the idea of God dwindled, man's spiritual significance also declined and now, instead of, as Wordsworth said,

". . . Trailing clouds of glory do we come
From God, who is our home."

it was said that man is merely a fortuitous aggrega-
tion of matter struck off by a mechanical universe. He
had no divine heritage and his immortal future was all
a gigantic delusion. We were informed that man is an
animal even if of a higher grade, an animal which
had learned to talk and do wonderful things with his
hands and brain, or perhaps he was only a miniature
machine of similar nature as the newly discovered
universe. To be sure, it was pointed out that it was
quite remarkable for animals or machines to write
plays like Shakespeare or music like Beethoven, but
the teachers of the new humanities blithely smiled
such objections away.

It was also urged that man did not readily yield to
the attempt to make a machine of him, for he still
possessed the two functions of a living organism—
namely, the ability to repair his own parts and to
reproduce himself. It was shown that no automobile,
for example, had been invented that could patch its
own tires, and that no case had been reported to the
Bureau of Vital Statistics where a happy Ford had
given birth to a litter of little Fords in some wondering garage.

God Is Dead? Antique Idea

Whereas at the turn of the century the great scientists were rather bowing God out of the universe, it now appears that under the influence of a more mature and therefore profounder knowledge of the natural sciences He is being ushered back with new respect into the world He made. It is becoming somewhat obvious, as a distinguished thinker has declared, "that if so much mind is required to read off the processes of the universe, it must itself be the product of mind." A universe once thought to be the result of a blind self-assembling of force and matter without benefit of a directing intelligence is a theory increasingly untenable to the modern mind.

Sir James Jeans, distinguished British scientific man, said that our universe seems to be more like a great thought than a great machine. Amplifying this opinion, he declared, "I would say as a speculation, not as a scientific fact, that the universe is a creation of some great universal mind underlying and coordinating all our minds," and he concludes, significantly, "Scientific knowledge seems to be moving in that direction."

Strangely enough, the minor thinkers have not yet quite comprehended this change of front in the scientific world. It would seem the profounder scientists are usually years in advance of the lesser teachers. The latter little realize how out of date they are with their simulated erudition and bored amusement. They wave aside what they consider the old, outworn spiritual view of man and his world. Meanwhile, the great thinkers have already restored the theistic belief to

an honored place in their cosmology. The small fry,
if past performance may truly prophesy, catch up with
this speeding truth at a slower pace—it takes about
twenty years. But sooner or later, people return like
the prodigal to belief in God and their own essential worth.

Greater Men Coming

It will conceivably be popular once again as in
days long gone to declaim to popular applause Shakespeare's noble lines, for these many years unhappily
in disuse: "What a piece of work is man!" Indeed,
Professor Whitehead, in his *Adventure of Ideas*, has
already led the way. "The importance of man," he
says, "as the supreme organism is beyond question.
With all his shortcomings in image, attribute, and deed
he deserves to be visited by Him who has ordained
the stars."

At this point warning should be given that, like
every other essential truth, the fact of man's greatness
may work itself out in forms beneficial to society or
in a manner subversive to human good. Stress on the
sovereignty of the individual and his potential powers
may lead to men like gods, investing all life with new
dignity and meaning, or to men, selfish and predatory.
It all depends upon the ideals that motivate these
greater personalities we are seeking to develop. An

unspiritual, non-religious, pagan philosophy of .individualism leads in the realm of thought to crass humanism, in the social order to ruthless Toryism, and in politics to the dictator. The important element in a renewed faith in man is the spiritualizing of his life and purpose.

Thus our point of view has in it the danger of creating dictators, but it also has the possibility of flowering out in men of great humanity like Schweitzer. It may make men who go for power and special privilege, but it may, if God touches them to release their greatness, make men to match the mountains, unselfish benefactors of humanity.

"God give us men," the poet once prayed, for, said he, "the time demands strong minds, great hearts. . . ." So it does, and only God can give those strong souls, who bless the world. An individualism without spiritual understanding is filled with dark and sinister possibilities.

When inspired by God, it becomes the salvation of our common life. Strong, good men, technicians of the secret of spiritual power, ever secure for themselves life's richest values, but more importantly they guarantee to all men the establishment of a social order of equity, justice, and enduring good will.

The sort of individualism I am advocating here is that which was in the mind of William James—"We and God have business with each other," he said, "and in that business our highest destiny is fulfilled."

Have a High Opinion of Yourself

It is therefore perfectly proper and in very good style for you to entertain a high opinion of yourself. Square your shoulders, and march forth bravely to meet life. You are more than a match for it. You are not going down to defeat. You are unconquerable. Not by your own merit, of course, but by the grace of God you may become the greatest being in God's world—and you must believe that; you can believe it.

There are many reliable sources to which we may turn for verification of this amazing assertion. The poets tell us it is true. They sing of the greatness of man. But the poet, alas, is not universally honored by a generation which has deified the practical man, he whose touch turns all to gold, or as sometimes happens, to debts and unemployment.

For some, the poet's songs seem to have wasted their sweetness on the desert air. The great poets are, however, the abiding seers of the human race. Their ears are more sensitive than ours. They hear the rich overtones of life where truth is whispered from high places. They have eyes with long-range vision, with power to penetrate to the essence of things through the dust of the streets which blind us whose sight, alas, is so faulty. It may be that in his brooding, a master poet is made ready for some illumination which comes finally, whereby in flashing insight he sees things as they are, even as a flash of lightning on a dark night reveals with cameolike distinctness a darkened landscape. As Guido in Browning's "Ring and the Book" saw Naples, its towers and steeples, and Vesuvius with its wisp of smoke on a stormy night etched for a flashing second before his gaze, so the poet once or twice in a lifetime beholds the glory of truth itself. He tells us of his vision in words that become immortal, less for their music than for truth which, Woodrow Wilson once pointed out in glorious phrase—"is no cripple; it can run alone."

Thus Tennyson, in "The Princess," in some of the most exquisite lines in English verse beholds the real value of you and me:

"The splendor falls on castle walls,
  And snowy summits old in story;
The long light shakes across the lakes.
  And wild cataract leaps in glory;
Blow, bugle, blow! set the wild echoes flying!
Blow, bugle! answer, echoes! dying, dying, dying."

This is the supernal beauty of the natural world, but time and decay will wear it down.

"O love, they die in yon rich sky.
  They faint on hill or field or river."

Not so with man; that fate will not overtake him sees the poet in ecstatic vision, and so he sings of the high, soaring triumph of man—

"Our echoes roll from soul to soul
And grow for ever and for ever."

You Are Greater Than You Think

That is what you are, the one great unbreakable, undefeatable creature in this universe. "The stars shall fade away, the sun himself grow dim with age," Addison tells us, but you "shall have eternal youth." What a figure you are! Standing at the center of a universe that waxes old like a garment, you alone are indestructible. As Dostoievski nobly expressed it, "We are citizens of eternity." Why, then, should you let the little things of daily life defeat you and destroy your strong effectiveness? Remember who you are. The world may look like Goliath, the giant, but you can defeat it for the simple reason that you are what you are, and that is enough.

But if the testimony of the poets is not convincing, let us hear from the men of science. They are, it appears, widely considered the oracles of our time. They inform us that we do not know half of our real value. We need and have the right to an enlarged conception of ourselves. Dr. Alexis Carrel, distinguished scientist and Nobel prize winner, turned away from those who entertain a low estimate of man. To Carrel, "despite its stupendous immensity, the world of matter is too narrow for him (man). Like his economic and social environment, it does not fit him. With the aid of mathematical abstractions his mind apprehends (and rules) electrons and stars. He is made on the scale of the terrestrial mountains, oceans, and rivers." It is you this great scientist is talking about.

Take a deep breath, for you are greater even than that, for Doctor Carrel is not yet through with you. "But he belongs also to another world. A world which, although enclosed within himself, stretches beyond space and time. And in this world, if his will is indomitable, he may travel over the infinite cycles." That is the latest word of modern science about what you are. Let a deep laugh well up within you at the grotesque idea that you ever believed life could defeat you.

The great philosophers must also be heard from on this important subject. What do they say about man? One of the supreme thinkers of modern times was Immanuel Kant. Through his brain passed some of the greatest thoughts ever entertained by the mind of man. He sums up all his great thoughts into just two which are expressed in a familiar passage: "Two things fill me with constantly increasing admiration and awe the longer and more earnestly I reflect on them, the starry heavens without and the moral law within." What did he mean by that? Simply that in each of us there is something in wonder and beauty comparable to the majesty and magnificence of the celestial vault. Can that be possible? Life bears it out.

Elevator Boy Braves Fire

I read of an elevator boy in a cheap hotel. He was only a kid off the streets and of doubtful parentage,

a bit of the flotsam and jetsam of life. In the dead of
night fire broke out in the upper stories of the hotel.
The stairway was soon cut off. The only way of
escape was the elevator. The boy ran his car tenta-
tively a time or two up into the burning hotel,
bringing down the terrified guests. The heat became
intense, the smoke blinding. He went up again and
came down with others. Should he go back for more?
Up above was fire and incredible heat and probable
injury, perhaps even death. He felt the cool air from
the street. Life was sweet to him. Why should he risk
his life? Nobody would expect it of him, for he was
only a waif. Why not make his escape?

But something within him resisted. He slammed the
door of his car and again and again shot up into that
hell of fire and flame until finally he went once too
often and the car became his funeral pyre. Was it not
the moral law within coming into its own, by which
life reaches its true level of equality with the stars
in their glory?

These poets and scientists and philosophers, testify-
ing to the greatness of you and me, remind us of a
Book written long ago. It is a Book designed to help
people know and realize themselves. In it we are told
that "God created man in his own image, . . . and
gave him dominion." The Book tells of a great Personality who touched men here and there and they
became men of power and strength. One of the men
helped by this Personality wrote about the power He
gives to those who believe in Him: "But as many as

received him, to them gave he power to become."
That is to say—this Personality helps them to become
what they have it in them to become.

Man in himself is not strong or great although he
possesses intrinsically the elements of greatness. When
in humility of spirit and by an act of surrender he
opens himself to the grace of God his Creator, then,
like a dynamo, ready for the power for which it was
made, he is attached to the source of an energy which
transforms him from mute ineffectiveness to creative
force.

In his famous address on "The Energies of Men"
William James declared, "Men habitually use only a
small part of the powers which they possess and which
they might use under appropriate circumstances."
A scientist is reported recently to have said that the
average man uses but twenty per cent of his brain
power. When you think of some people, that sounds
like optimism. Think of it—you are using, if you are an
average person, only one fifth of your mental capacity.

Consider what you could make of life if you increased
that only fifty per cent. In the personality of every
individual is a great reservoir of unused power. But
in many of us just a miserable little trickle is getting
through, and on that we live and do our work. The
great secret of life is to put a key into the lock, turn
back the sluice gates and let that power, like a terrific stream, flow into your mind and personality,
transforming you into a person of strength and ef-

fectiveness, well able to meet and master all circumstances.

Applied Christianity helps people to tap this reservoir of power within themselves. I have seen it work so astoundingly in so many lives that I have come to believe that the man who will not use this power so freely available to him is as foolish as a man who, knowing that oil is in his back yard, refuses to sink a well and instead goes on living from hand to mouth. That is exactly what is done by people who, knowing of the power real Christianity holds, refuse to let it into their lives.

Of course, I realize that much Christianity as preached and practiced fails to reveal this power. It has been made a lifeless thing of creed and ceremony, and stereotyped jargon and allowed to be considered a system of social ethics only. Christianity is not a creed to be recited but a power to be tapped. Nor is it only a social bill of rights, although it is that in every sense of the phrase. The important thing to emphasize is that it is a source of inward power by which weak personalities can become strong; divided personalities can become unified; hurt minds can be healed; and the secret of peace and poise attained.

Every Weakness Can Be Cured

There is no weakness or illness of personality that cannot be cured by applied Christianity. The science

of psychology is revealing the wonder and possibility
of human personality, just as exploration in early days
opened up the possibilities of the physical world. One
great fact growing out of it is the absolute and amazing results in becoming bigger and better and stronger
personalities, to be obtained through faith in and practice of the spirit and presence of Christ. Thoughtful
men today are learning the validity of the experience
of a man named Paul, who, himself a divided personality, met Christ and ever afterward went about
saying a wonderful thing: "I can do all things through
Christ who giveth me the strength." The strange
power found by the sage of Tarsus long ago is still
available for any man who is wise enough to want
this power and who will take it. To meet Christ in
this sense is to meet yourself for the first time in your
life, and you will be happier with the new self than
the old, for now you will begin truly to live.

I was speaking one night along this line, and at the
close I noticed a young woman waiting for me in
obvious agitation. As soon as she saw that I was un-
occupied she approached and with great intensity
asked, "For God's sake, can you do anything for me?"
She was a handsome young woman, stylishly dressed.
It was evident that she had been drinking to excess.
My reply was, "No, I cannot do much for you but I
can introduce you to Someone who can do for you
anything that needs to be done." I asked her to go
into my office, where she told her story.

She had come of a good family and was a graduate

of high school and college, in both cases with honors.
Her training was religious and idealistic. She had married, but the marriage had failed and a divorce had
eventuated. Her earlier ideals of life became blunted
as she acquiesced finally in the loose morality of the
times. It brought her no happiness but, on the contrary, increased the dissatisfaction and misery of her
life. Her mind fell into a state of bewildered confusion
and she was assailed by an overwhelming repulsion
and disgust. When I saw her, she was, to use her own
phrase, "at the end of a shabby rope." "No," I said,
in the quiet of my office, "there is little I can do for
you but I will make you a proposition if you really
want help." I then told her that if she would completely surrender her life in every respect to Jesus
Christ and take the power He would give her in return, she would enter into an altogether new life.

She asked, "How do you surrender?" To which I
replied, "Just say to Christ, 'I give my life into Your
hands.'" Again she questioned, "How can I take the
power He offers?" For answer I picked up a book
and held it out to her. "Take it," I said, "it is as simple as that." She did these things as simply as a child,
this sophisticated, ultramodern girl. There in the office
of a Fifth Avenue church the ancient miracle repeated
itself whereby Christ touched a life and it was changed,
really changed. She became, to use the words of the
New Testament, "a new creature." It was real too. In
the years that have passed since that night she has
become happy, strong, and good. Life, no longer near

the shallows, is at high tide for her now. Only vital
Christianity can perform a service like that. Other
forces have been invented or discovered which can
change the face of nature, but only this kind of Christianity can transform human nature.

Some people may doubt an experience like this, or
explain it away on psychological grounds, or smile it
away as old-fashioned evangelism. But that has no effect on my thinking for I am not speculating in theories. I am merely stating events that I have witnessed
and know to be facts. No man can argue away a fact.
It is because these facts were known to be true that
we can say positively that any person who is not satisfied with his life and wants a better one can have it
by the method outlined in this chapter and throughout this book. This guarantee is absolute and un-
qualified and may be and is supported by the prag-
matic slogan, "Ask the man who has experienced it."

Two

HOW TO GET RID OF WORRY

Life for most people would be happy and satisfying if they could overcome worry. If by some miracle one could be assured that he need never worry again, it would seem like an altogether new world. That assurance we mean to offer in this chapter. It is both right and possible that worry should be eliminated from your life.

One of the first things we must do in learning the art of living is to have a funeral service. There is a certain old fellow who should be buried under six feet of earth with no monument to do him honor. Possibly he is in your house even now as you read this book and is sitting by your side. Look around and see if he is there. I am referring to Old Man Worry. What a character he is! Just look at him and study him well. Perhaps you have never really scrutinized him before.

There he sits with his wrinkled brows, thin lips, and sharp, bloodless features. He has a nervous, rasping laugh, devoid of mirth. He has sunken cheeks and a shifting, anxious look in his deep-set eyes. He is a cadaverous old fellow with icy fingers and a cold, clammy breath. He is sitting there with you even though he knows how you abhor him. You have allowed him to think he is your master, and he exercises his authority to the full. After awhile you will go to bed and the old fellow will shamble into your bedroom with you. He will sit there and keep you awake for a long time, and after a troubled sleep, when you awaken in the morning, the first thing to greet you will be the sardonic face of Old Man Worry.

When you go to your office or to your shop or store or to the fields, he will go along with you. All day long he will be your constant companion. Perhaps when evening comes, you will go out with friends and will manage to forget him for a space, losing yourself in the gaiety of pleasant companionship; but just when you are becoming light-hearted and gay, suddenly you will feel a cold breath and, looking around, will see him, Old Man Worry, at your elbow.

Something must be done about this old character if you are to live and be happy.

Chuck Old Man Worry

My suggestion is that you put down this volume, get to your feet, ceremonially walk over and open the door wide and invite him firmly and none too politely to get out and stay out forever. If he will not go of his

own accord, take him by the nape of the neck and
eject him forcibly. Throw him as hard as you can. His
old bones are brittle and if you do it with righteous
determination and the attitude of a man throwing off
a tyrant, you will never be troubled with him again.
This may sound like a bit of very curious advice, but
worry can never be handled effectively in any other
way than by dealing with it forthrightly. Without
making up your mind to get through with it as long
as one nurses it along, hating it yet compromising
with it, worry will remain with you. There must come
a time when you will rise up in your full determination and say decisively, "Old Man Worry must go. As
far as I'm concerned, I've had it with worry."

Why should we be so bitter against this old fellow
whom you are ejecting from your life? Simply because
worry makes people unhappy, and the good God never
meant that His children should be unhappy. We have a
beautiful world in which to live, where generous provision is made for our joy. Did not Browning remind
us that "There's a world of capability for joy spread
round about us, meant for us, inviting us"?

Difficulty, stiff and stern, is here, of course, for the
wise Creator knew full well that men could not be
happy in any easy universe. Struggle makes for strength
and the deep satisfaction of achievement. Nature does
not yield her benefits cheaply. She insists that man
shall gain them by mental agony and the sweat of his
brow, but the struggle is fair and clean and rich in
satisfaction. Man usually makes his own unhappiness.

Christian, the Englishman, and the Tahiti girl were exploring *Pitcairn's Island*,[1] as recorded in that epic story. Maimiti of a sudden halted. "There have been people here before us," she said.

"Here? Nonsense, Maimiti! What makes you think so?"

"I know it," she replied, gravely. "It must have been long ago, but there was only a path where we are now walking."

Christian smiled incredulously. "I can't believe it," he said.

"Because you are not of our blood," the girl replied. "But Moitua would know or Minarii. I felt this as we were climbing up from the landing place. Now I am sure of it. People of my own race have lived here at some time."

"Why have they gone then?"

"Who knows?" she replied. "Perhaps it is not a happy place."

"Not happy, an island so rich and beautiful?"

"The people may have brought some old unhappiness with them. It is not often the land that is to blame; it is those who come."

Thus worry comes into man's life, a foreign element, which has no legitimate right to be there and which for his peace and well-being must be removed.

By the term "worry" we do not, of course, mean a wise and normal concern but, rather, that nervous

[1] By Nordhoff and Hall. Reprinted by permission of Little Brown & Company.

feeling of impending trouble which, in turn, gives rise
to stress and tension with their attendant ills. Worry
lays upon life burdens that it was never meant to bear
and casts deep and unnatural shadows upon the spirit
of man. God surely intended man to live a Garden-
of-Eden existence but by his perversity he lost his
citizenship in that happy country. Fortunately, there
is a road back to Eden for those who seek it with a
whole heart. A buoyant, childlike happiness is man's
rightful heritage, and it lies at the foot of no illusory
rainbow, but under his own doorstep in the true country of the spirit from whence, foolish man, he departed
to look in false directions for life's good.

Worry Undermines Health

Another reason for our determination to wage war
against worry is because of what it does to people
physically. Some years ago the commissioner of health
of the City of New York issued a booklet bearing the
title, *Man's Danger Line Begins at Forty*, implying that
life may truly begin at that age if men would early
learn to prevent diseases that come with middle age.
The commissioner offered eleven rules for the preven-
tion of serious disease, and heading the list is this
primary suggestion, "For one less hour of worry sub-
stitute one more hour of laughter." Physical breakdown
is not caused by either the amount or the importance
of work but, rather, by anxiety and worry which, when

added to one's responsibilities, overload the nervous system to the point of danger.

As long as one does his work with poise and unhurried attitude, properly balancing labor and rest, maintaining at the same time a confident, simple faith, his duties will be lightly borne and each night will find him with unalloyed satisfaction for a reward. Let him add worry and anxiety and the spell is broken. Tension creates a new stress and strain. The element of panic in even small degree destroys the power to relax either mentally or physically, with the commonly known results to the circulatory and nervous systems.

Heart trouble, high blood pressure, and nervous breakdown are afflictions of such universality that one seemingly must almost have one or all of them to be in style in this hectic year of our Lord. Life's unnaturally increased tempo affects a person's ability to think in calm and orderly fashion, and consequently the quality of his work is adversely affected. He becomes either foolhardy and unwise or cautious and hesitant, losing both the balance of restraint and the psychology of attack. In either case he has lost that firm control which is the requisite to success and to mental and spiritual well-being. The man who worries will usually not go forward. Timorousness holds him back. The men who do things just do things. But if they worried about doing things, they would never do things.

Real Faith Can Heal

I called upon an eminent physician, himself a patient in a New York hospital. In the course of our conversation I asked why he was there. He replied that he had a physical malady which was directly the cause of worry. "When I worry," he said, "this physical problem arises and I am forced to come here for several weeks. But when I get hold of myself and stop worrying, I get well and go about my work." Then he added this significant bit of advice, "Teach your people not to worry but to trust God and have faith and you will keep many of them out of the hospitals and away from the doctors."

Wise physicians of the body know that out of the mind are most of the issues of health, and that a peaceful mind is the best medicine one can take. The current years of financial, social, and international upheaval have greatly added to physical maladjustments, and worry has been a major contributing factor. Men have gone to pieces physically, mentally, and spiritually because of worry over conditions as they are affected by them. The effect upon health has been marked. The problem of worry and its relation to the well-being of people, always an important one, has become greatly accentuated. People rush here and there, seeking cures, taking health baths, and calling upon the benevolent ray to save them. The helpfulness of such methods is not to be questioned, but no out-

ward treatment can cure an inward condition. It does
no good to spray rose water on a cancer. The solution is to bring unified adjustment, inner peace and
harmony to the mind—in other words, put an end to
the worry which is the principal cause of the outward
physical manifestations.

In a New York club the physical director told me
of the many men, upset and nervous, who come to
him for therapeutic treatment, and of the marked
increase in cases of ill health in recent years; most of
them, he confided, the result of worry. Himself no
churchman, nor even formally religious, he told me
that instead of paying five or ten dollars a treatment
they would do better to spend, as he said, "a few
dollars for a Bible and read the New Testament for
thirty minutes each night and morning." He informed
me that on several occasions he had gone so far as
to prescribe this method of treatment for some of his
astonished patients.

His theory was, of course, that physical ailments,
when related to nervous disturbances, will yield to the
peace which faith in God develops. The healing value
of religious faith in cases where the background is
one of nervous tension is demonstrated daily. There is
in the New Testament a definite spiritual technique for
such healing; in essence it is contained in the formula,
"Thou wilt keep him in perfect peace whose mind is
stayed on thee."

But we are anticipating the cure for worry which
we set out to suggest. We have seen the deleterious

effects of worry and have promised to suggest how
worry may be banished from the mind. Now for an
answer to the question, and here it is in simple and
succinct form.

The first thing is to practice a new attitude of mind:
practice because it cannot be developed at once. It
requires long and persistent cultivation. Adopt the
attitude of dwelling upon your blessings instead of
your troubles, especially the ones which have not happened but which you anticipate with worry. Even the
man who seems to be in a sea of troubles can find
some things to be thankful for.

Don't Build Up Your Troubles

Troubles have a way of assuming undue proportions,
and even a small difficulty can so magnify itself that
the entire landscape of one's life is dominated by it.
He is, you might say, a pompous tough guy, vaunting
himself like a little man with an inferiority complex,
who finds his defense in assuming larger proportions
than he merits. Usually the person who worries reflects
so constantly upon his troubles, those he has and those
he expects, that his whole sky seems dark and gloomy.
Now let him begin to affirm and dwell upon the good
things in his life and he will find them better company. They are more modest and do not intrude themselves nor become assertive until they are made by
continued association to feel at home. But when that

time comes, how they seem to increase in numbers
and their glad voices make the old, dreary house of a
man's mind a cheery place once more! Herein lies the
secret of effectiveness in living.

A sales manager in a large company was faced
with the problem of declining sales by some of his
representatives. He called them in to the home office
for a conference, which was very short and simple.
On the wall he had tacked a large sheet of white
paper, in the center of which he had placed a black
dot. He asked each salesman in turn what he saw
on the paper and each replied, "A black dot." When
he had gone the rounds, he asked, "Now, does any
man here see anything on the paper but a black dot?"
In concert and individually they all affirmed that they
could see only a black dot. The sales manager said,
"Can't any of you see the white space on the paper?"
and added: "That is the trouble with you men. You
can see only the black dot and you miss the extensive
white space where there are no black dots."

Then he told them to go back to their territories
and look for the white space, for the opportunities that
were there. There may be in your life many black
dots, but never forget there is also a large amount of
white space, and it behooves us to form the habit of
mind by which we look for the good instead of the
bad, for opportunities rather than difficulties. The final
result will be to restore life to its true proportions
and relieve us from the foolishness of worry.

This leads to a second suggestion, which is to re-cover the great virtue of common sense in dealing with worry. Common sense is an important virtue to possess. Despite its name, it is really all too uncommon. It teaches us one great thing—that by far the largest share of our worries is unjustified. Think through your experience and see if that is not true. Actually most of the troubles we have worried about in the past never happened. Life averages well, which means that most of the troubles we are worrying about now will never happen. Emerson, who has often been termed and not inappropriately "the wisest American," ex-pressed the falsity of anticipated worries:

"Some of your hurts you have cured,
    And the sharpest you still have survived,
But what torments of grief you endured
    From evils which never arrived!"

Learn to Shut the Gate

We worry likewise about decisions made in the past. Now, really, what good is it to worry about a decision that has been made? For good or ill it is made, so why not put it out of mind? If it was wrong, charge it up to experience. If it was right, thank God for your wisdom. But, good or bad, shut the gate on it. Lloyd George, playing golf with a friend, went through a pasture gate. The friend, who was following, left the gate open, whereupon the war premier turned about and closed it, saying, "I have always made it a practice to close a gate when I have passed through it."

That is a very good rule for those who desire peace of mind. Shut the gate and keep it shut and your worries cannot follow you. People who worry about things that never happen remind me of a good woman I knew in my childhood who for sixty years had looked under the bed every night for a burglar she never found. I always wondered what she would have done if she had at last found one. She would probably have died of shock, not at seeing a burglar but of surprise that one finally was there.

Set your worries down on paper, those that have happened and those that have not happened, and I will venture the opinion that for most of us the latter greatly outnumber the former. It would be a wholesome idea to frame that paper where you can see it when you retire each night. It will help you to sleep well, and in the morning it will give you courage and faith for the day.

I remember a friend, a wonderful, wise old man, who was one of the happiest personalities I knew anywhere. His life had not been an easy one, and he had known many real hardships and difficulties. I often wondered as to the secret of his happiness and peace of mind. That secret is revealed in a little poem which he wrote and which we would all do well to give a place in our philosophy of life.

"Better never trouble trouble
　Until trouble troubles you,
For you're sure to make your trouble
　Double trouble when you do.
And your trouble, like a bubble,
　That you're troubling about,
May be nothing but a cipher
　With the rim rubbed out." [1]

What About Real Concerns?

But what about those worries having a real foundation? What shall we say to the man who is unem-
ployed, his reserves fast dwindling if not already gone,
and who, against his will, must accept governmental
relief? Some practical suggestion must be given to the
businessman who faces a very real possibility of failure
by reason of existing conditions. The mother whose
children are no imaginary source of concern cannot
be told that her worries are without basis in fact.
The answer to these and all of life's real difficulties
is threefold.

The first is that common sense is an aid here, also,
for the man who possesses it knows that he must have
a mind free of worry if he is to meet difficulty effectively. A cool, steady, unflustered mind is a quality
greatly to be desired. One must have all his faculties
unimpaired and going for him to meet real problems
squarely. The second answer to the problems of factual

[1] Dr. David Keppel.

worry, especially those created by economic and social causes beyond the control of the individual, is that worry will not correct them. We must study better social control and unremittingly seek to reorganize our social order in such a way that justice will guarantee to each worthy person his proportionate share of economic good and opportunity.

There is a third solution to the problem of worry, however, and here we discover a priceless secret. There is nothing that will so completely guarantee the banishment of worry as the attitude of faith and trust in the goodness and the caring character of God. Many people fail at this point because they do not acquire the simple technique involved in faith and trust. They unfortunately think it means intellectual adherence to the historic propositions of the Christian faith. This is not a matter of dependence upon an idea, but upon a Person, a Person who cares.

It is an instinctive rather than a reasoned trust, although it will bear the weight of logic. It is for a person to say: "I believe God is good—that He is a kindly Father. And because He is that He will not forget me nor let me be defeated." Such a man will sincerely do his best to secure a living for himself and his dependents. He will not sit down and wait for God to supply his needs miraculously but will exercise ingenuity and resourcefulness to the fullest extent in his own behalf. All the time, however, there will be in his mind a calm conviction that a fair and kindly Providence will sustain him. He will build his faith on an assurance from the Bible, like this—"God shall supply all our need."

The God of Supply

But one may ask—"You said that God would satisfy all my needs. How about my economic needs?" And I answer unhesitatingly that the promise covers that also. Of course, it does not mean that the lazy man shall receive any help from God. He doesn't deserve it. The man who leans on a shovel cannot expect to lean on God. But the person who honestly tries his dead level best will find that all of the forces of the universe will endeavor to assist him. No time is too hard for God, no situation too difficult. God helps people economically in different ways. One of the ways is to inspire them to work for a better social order so that such difficulties as we face socially will, in the future, be impossible. But quite apart from that there is an old passage in the Bible which is gloriously true—"I have been young, and now am old; yet have I not seen the righteous forsaken, nor his seed begging bread."

My church is situated at the heart of New York City, and month after month we deal with people who are economically hard pressed. Sometimes they have to go through some hard times, but I will say that in these years I have never yet seen a worthy, honest man permanently defeated. How it happens I do not know, but ultimately God takes care of them,

even financially. That is a bold thing to say, but I
could recite case after case where absolute and sincere
faith in God's guidance and watchful care has been
abundantly rewarded.

These are people, however, who have completely—
and I mean completely, not half-heartedly—surrendered
themselves to the will of God. They have said: "Lord,
I put my life in Your hands. I know You will take
care of me." Where they have taken that attitude
toward God, the wonderful thing has happened. He
has poured into them His own power. He gives them
fresh insight and new ideas. They have discovered,
indeed, that He satisfies all their needs. The essential
thing here is the sort of faith a small child has in the
protective love and helpful kindliness of his father.

Take a Cue from the Birds

As I write, an illustration of this truth is being
enacted before my eyes. I look out from a hotel
window to the famous Atlantic City Boardwalk. There
has been a protracted spell of intensely cold weather.
The waters of the back bay are frozen solid and the
sea gulls are deprived of their usual source of food
supply. For hours this morning the snow-covered beach
has been gray with hundreds of gulls waiting for twelve
o'clock and feeding time. Now comes a man wheeling
a barrel of scraps down to the beach, where he spreads
it upon the snowy sands and with hoarse, glad cries

the multitude of birds are fed. The birds have learned to know there is human kindness which is concerned for their plight. Theirs not to reason how or why; they only know at the appointed hour a wise and kindly friend will care for them.

So we often sit by a cold, winter sea and the storm and ice invade our lives. Our sources of provision are closed and worry and anxiety grip us with chilling thoughts. But then, if we have the child-like heart of faith, we can hear a voice telling us something about no bird falling from heaven unnoticed by our Heavenly Father and that our very hairs are numbered. The voice tells us to take no thought for the morrow, meaning to have no worried thought about tomorrow, for our Father knows our needs. Of course, some minds are so very adult, or shall we say sophisticated, that the voice seems too good to be true, but to the man who can still make of himself a little child, it means everything, and he finds it not false but fabulously true.

Once a great poet of the Southland stood watching the birds building nests on the uncertain marshes. He was a real sufferer, walking in his own dark valley. On the desolate marsh he watched the trusting little marsh-hen building a nest to rear her young. She sang notes of happiness. She was not afraid. Some instinct deep in her feathered bosom told her an eternal kindness watched over her. Sidney Lanier learned the lesson for himself and sings it for us:

"As the marsh-hen secretly builds on the watery sod,
Behold I will build me a nest on the greatness of God:
I will fly in the greatness of God as the marsh-hen flies
In the freedom that fills all the space 'twixt the marsh
    and the skies:
By so many roots as the marsh-grass sends in the sod
I will heartily lay me a-hold on the greatness of God:
Oh, like to the greatness of God is the greatness within
The range of the marshes, the liberal marshes of Glynn."

Three

TAKING TIME TO LIVE

When Mrs. Ramsay MacDonald, wife of a former British prime minister, was dying, she called her husband to her bedside for a last word. "Keep romance in the lives of our children," she admonished him. It was an impressive parting message which, as we reflect upon it, is deep with wisdom.

This mother knew, as all who meditate seriously upon life must know, that the passing years make a terrific assault upon the zest of man's spirit, and unless he exercises care, will steal from him the romance of life. Napoleon said, "Men grow old quickly on the battlefield"—they do in life also unless they are vigilant.

Charles Lamb once declared, "Our spirits grow gray before our hairs." One starts out in youth with anticipation. Excitedly he looks down the approaching years with the spirit of an adventurer, but before he has traveled far life starts blowing its cold winds upon him. He tries his wings, perhaps they fail him; and some, sadly enough, having been disillusioned a time

47

or two, give over the dreams and plod wearily on over a pathway from which the romance has fled. That is one of the saddest things that can happen to anyone, to lose the thrill and zest of living.

There is one certain way to decide whether you are old—namely, what is your attitude of mind when you arise in the morning? The person who is young awakes with a strange feeling of excitement, a feeling which he may not be able to explain but which is as if to say, "This is the great day; this is the day on which the wonderful thing will happen." The individual who is old, regardless of age, arises with the spirit unresponsive, not expecting any great thing to happen. This day will be just about like all the rest. They may hope it will be no worse. Some people retain the spirit of expectation at threescore and ten; some lose it early in life. The measure of one's age is actually how well he retains the romance of life.

Perhaps Wordsworth gave us the best description of the sad process that takes place in many:

> "Heaven lies about us in our infancy
> Shades of the prison-house begin to close
>   Upon the growing boy,
> But he beholds the light, and whence it flows,
>   He sees it in his joy;
> The youth, who daily farther from the east
>   Must travel, still is Nature's priest
>   And by the vision splendid
>   Is on his way attended;
> At length the man perceives it die away,
> And fade into the light of common day."

The romance of life is so priceless a possession that it is a supreme tragedy to lose it. Though one may acquire much in wealth, fame, or honor, the real joy of life does not lie there but, rather, in keeping the romance of living going. Nothing gives such complete and profound happiness as the perpetually fresh wonder and mystery of exciting life.

Train Whistles Among the Hills

When I was a small boy, I lay in bed at night and heard the long, low whistle of the train among the hills of southern Ohio. I could see in imagination the speeding train, with its brightly lighted cars, whisking through the night. I always used to love a train and to me there was no more thrilling sight than a big express train speeding over a countryside brightly silhouetted against the darkness. The chief ambition of my boyhood days was to be a railroad engineer. I am thankful that such things still thrill me. When these thrills pass, the romance of life is on the way out.

How quickly for some people the freshness of life passes away! The work to which we set ourselves with high hopes and intense interest is allowed to degenerate into dreary monotony. The marriage begun with such bliss becomes commonplace in the steady round of day-by-day living. The hopes and ambitions which once stirred us become lifeless. Far horizons no longer beckon. The joy of life has fled, leaving our days hollow and our activity meaningless. What shall we do?

What do people generally do when they discover that the excitement of life is going or is gone? Many turn completely to material things as the possible source of its recovery. They think that if they can just possess more things, have more money, enjoy more privileges, go more places, the old joy in life will return. Others turn to a pleasure program when they find the romance of life growing dull. By new sensations, they argue, they will regain life's thrill. They forget that one thrill calls for another in endless succession until a person loses his sensitive appreciation of the beautiful and becomes calloused and cynical.

Still others hope to recapture it by casting aside all restraint and ideals. The trouble with that method is that sensations wear out and become jaded. Also, by-pass it as we will, everyone has a troublesome little affair in him called the conscience, which is easily hurt, and a pain in that area is hard to cure. Moreover, in every man, given him by nature, is an innate self-respect which, while it may not prevent him from doing evil, will keep him from ever having peace after he succumbs to evil.

How to Keep Romance in Living

There are others—honest, wholesome people—who just bravely accept the dreariness of life's hardships. They have too much sense to seek departed romance

in things and also too much honor and wisdom to turn
to sensual pleasure. But some fortunate people have
found the true method of keeping romance in life.
There was Robert Louis Stevenson, confined to a bed
of pain through long years, yet able to write such
happy, lilting little verses that children everywhere
have been made joyous by them.

> "The children sing in far Japan;
> The children sing in Spain;
> The organ and the organ man
> Are singing in the rain."

Stevenson himself knew how to sing in the rain.

All of which brings us to the fact we want to emphasize, that the secret of a successful and happy life
consists in taking time to live. Life is an art, and to
be successful in any art it is necessary to know the
real from the imitation and to be content only with
fineness of quality. The tragic fact is that many people
are content with imitation life when they could just
as easily possess the genuine.

In *The Barretts of Wimpole Street* Elizabeth Barrett
Browning thoughtfully protests, "What frightens me
is that men are content with what is not life at all."
She is right about many of us. We pass hastily through
restless, hurried, anxious days and call it living, thinking if we capture a vagrant thrill now and then that
it is life. Deep in our hearts, however, we know that
real life is better than that; it is a great and wonderful
experience which is to be fervently desired.

Don't Let Busyness Get You

The time in which we live has made real life difficult, but as we shall see, far from impossible. We are a generation busy with things. Stevenson wrote, "The world is so full of a number of things; I am sure we should all be as happy as kings." The world has many more things than in Stevenson's day but there is grave doubt if their possession has really solved the problem of happiness. I can push buttons all over my house and have light, music, and heat. My grandfather had no buttons to push, but just the same he knew the art of living. He was a happy man. The increase of things, instead of providing leisure to be enjoyed, in all too many cases has but multiplied our confusion.

If Wordsworth, in the quiet of the English Lake Country, could say years ago, "The world is too much with us," what would he say now in modern America? We are also a generation of busyness. Hurry and speed drive us on. A large billboard near the outskirts of a Middle Western city proclaims, "This is a city of wings and wheels." So is most every city. We have the green-light psychology—not that we must make the green light, but how terrible to wait through the red! Watch people waiting for the light to change. Notice that tense expression. That is one thing wrong with us.

All of this has had unfortunate physical effects. It has made nerves and high blood pressure and heart trouble widespread. In speaking of the physical and nervous effects of hurry, William James said, "Neither

the nature nor the amount of our work is account-
able for the frequency and severity of our breakdowns.
But their cause lies, rather, in that absurd feeling of
hurry and having no time, in breathlessness and tension and anxiety."

This has done something even more serious to modern people. I refer to its deep psychological and cultural effects. It has had a tendency to make us superficial and thus incapable of appreciating the deeper
and more subtle values. This hectic, hasty, hurrying
age of ours has left the average man bewildered and
out of breath. It has made him think that the chief
virtue is to keep up with the flying clock. We seem
to have the idea that everyone must be constantly
doing something. One must be driving a car or danc-
ing or playing bridge or golf or going to the theater
or doing something. The American people—and that
means you and me—greatly need to learn to reduce
life's tempo unless we are to allow this hurly-burly
space age to rob us of life's deepest meaning and
happiness.

Take It Easy

A story is told of some Americans who were making
their way through Africa. They had employed a group
of natives at the seaport and had told them they were
in a great hurry, as Americans usually are. The first
day they went with rapid progress through the jungle.
They continued the relentless pace the second day. The

third morning, when they were hurriedly preparing
for another day of rapid travel, they found the savages
squatting under the trees and refusing to move. When
their bewildered and helpless employers asked them
why they were not ready to start, they said simply,
"We shall rest today to let our souls catch up with
our bodies."

Our failure to take time to live actually prevents us
from deriving the best from life. Man assuredly was
never meant by the good God to beat out his life in
hurry and tumult, wearing out his nervous system and
making his inner life shabby. We are given this world
to live in happily and reflectively. Let us take time
to live. Many of us were brought up on the books of
Horatio Alger. One bore the title: *Strive and Succeed.*
That point of view has been carried to an extreme.
Good, hard work is one of man's greatest boons, and
a lazy man is to be pitied. But perhaps we will succeed better if we strive less or, at least, reduce the
tension of our effort. What good is it anyway to succeed if one cannot enjoy life in the process? We are
missing the secret of happy life in this modern American spirit of hurry.

One of the practical contributions the spiritual view
makes to the happiness of everyday life is that it
shows the pleasure in simple things. Here again is
revealed the wisdom of Jesus. The sophisticate says
one must have thrills constantly reactivated to enjoy
life, little realizing that thrills pass away or at least

become jaded, ever requiring new stimulation, until finally one is more than likely to become fed up.

Christianity, on the other hand, directs attention to those basic things which wear well and make life increasingly interesting. How foolish people are to place so great emphasis on perishables which soon get stale instead of perpetually enjoying those delights of the mind and spirit which do not wear out, but grow more exciting with every passing year!

Taking time to live, then, means to realize that the supreme values of this world are spiritual things like music, art, literature, nature and religion. Many people, especially hard-pressed business men, feel mistakenly that music and art and books and religion are not as pressingly important as the mass of details with which their lives are filled. Such men will find themselves becoming a mere machine, whereas God designed each one to be a man. It is well to remember that we do not primarily live to work. We work to live. A person who spends his life with details as the chief concern misses the mark and dies a failure no matter what success he attains. He never learned the skill of life organization.

Stop Starving Your Spirit

Do not be a slave to life's machinery; get a song, a lovely poem, and the whisper of God's voice into your mind. You may not know it, but I will tell you

honestly that you are starved for these things, and the
worst kind of hunger is the longing of man's soul for
the things that are more nourishing than bread. No
wiser thing was ever said than that statement of the
great Thinker, Jesus: "Man does not live by bread
alone." He lives, instead, by the beauty of nature, by
music and art, and supremely by the presence of the
eternal.

I, a city dweller, once had a summer place on a
cedar-crested bluff overlooking a lovely bay down by
the sea. The salt breezes off the mighty ocean swept
cares away; the soft sunlight falling on the grass taught
the quiet repose of earth; the unhurried sounds of the
natural world, so different in quality from strident
city noises. These quieted me as a mother soothes her
troubled child; and at night when the stars came out,
blossoming one by one in the infinite meadows of
heaven, and a hush fell over land and sea, I could
hear the friendly voice of Mother Nature, which is
the voice of God, saying: "My child, this is life. Take
time to live it."

Make Good Friends

Taking time to live also means to cultivate friend-
ships. Shakespeare advised us to bind our friends to
us as with hoops of steel. Mark Twain reminded us
that good books and good friends make up the ideal
life. We are less than smart to permit the business of

life to keep us from the happiness of creative friend-
ships.

I learned a good lesson once from a happy Irish-
man. It was in Dublin, Ireland, where I called to see
a leading merchant of that city. I found a large and
very busy department store, and surrounded with all
the details of its administration was the man I had
come to see. Seeing he was busy, I tried after a brief
greeting, to excuse myself, but he asked me to wait and
in a few minutes reappeared with his hat. Soon we
were seated in his car and he was enthusiastically
showing me the sights of the city. When I remarked
at his courtesy in leaving his work to be so gracious to
me, he said in his big voice, "Not a bit of it, not a
bit of it; I never overlook the chance to make a new
friend, and, besides"—and this struck me—"I am running the store; the store isn't running me." This man
knew how to live and his spirit showed it.

The business of cultivating friends also suggests the
thought that God intended us to find interest and
fellowship in people. We are unfortunately so exces-
sively taken up with ourselves and the technique of
our days that we miss the rare delight of learning to
know better all sorts and conditions of men. It is
rewarding to cultivate the habit of looking for the
interesting qualities in people. There is something
interesting in every person.

Look at the man across from you on the bus or
subway—ordinary looking enough, isn't he? Yes, but

if you only knew the drama, the tragedy, the comedy, even the glory and heroism in that man's life, he would be full of interest to you. Some of the greatest books ever written are about simple, everyday people and simple, everyday happenings. The genius of Charles Dickens, and other enduring writers, is to be found in their ability to see the dramatic quality in what is often mistakenly called commonplace life. There is no such thing as commonplace life.

Painting on a Barrel Head

In Florence, Italy, I saw the painting by Raphael called "The Madonna of the Barrel." The outline of the head of a barrel in lieu of canvas is plainly discernible. The story is that Raphael was walking one day through the market place of Florence when he saw a mother, evidently a very poor woman, sitting in the street with her child at her breast. She was dressed in shabby attire but on her face was the ineffable expression of mother love. Raphael was so charmed by her appearance that nothing would do but that he must paint her at once and where she sat.

Accordingly, he took for his canvas the head of an old barrel which was conveniently near by, and using color and brushes which were in his pocket painted on the barrel head a picture which today hangs in one of the galleries of Florence, a masterpiece. Raphael was an immortal artist by reason of his native gifts, but more than that because of his capacity to see the beautiful and the romantic in everyday people, even a poor woman in a market place.

How can we dully complain that life has lost interest? Look upon the face of that dear one near you; hear the happy laughter of that little child; really know your fellow men. Life will never lose its romance for the person who, unselfishly, does good for people. Those who do lose the thrill of living are the ones who develop the habit of thinking exclusively about themselves, who are constantly concerned with their own interests or their own pleasures, or, what is more common, their own troubles. Start the habit of doing good to the people nearest you. This policy will make you so happy that you will sing inside, and the whole world about you will take on richer color. The grass will be greener; the songs of the birds will be sweeter; the stars will be brighter; the skies bluer; and even if the bank account is low and things are tough, the dreariness of life will depart if you learn the secret of finding your happiness in human service.

I have often heard my father relate the following incident, of which he was an eyewitness, as illustrating how human kindliness and helpfulness can develop a happy and exciting life. The man about whom this story is told was a great expert in the art of living and by his personality impressively showed the technique of that art to his students, who have not forgotten it after many years.

Johnny the Newsboy

In a mid-Western city some years ago was a great surgeon who was also a professor in the medical school. This surgeon was a true physician in that he not only had superlative skills but also loved people and went about doing good. He became deeply interested in the little crippled newsboy at the corner, where the doctor regularly bought his paper. He was a bright little fellow, this newsboy, and the famous surgeon said to him one day, "Johnny, would you like to have me cure that leg of yours so that you could run and play like other boys?" "Oh, Doctor," said the little lad, "that would make me so happy!"

Accordingly, the surgeon arranged to operate upon the boy and explained to him that he wanted to perform the operation in the presence of his class of medical students to teach the students how to help other little boys when they became doctors. Johnny agreed. He was placed before the surgeon and the students were arranged in tiers as in an amphitheater so that they could witness the operation. The doctor explained the disease and operative procedure he was to follow.

When all was ready, he said, "Now, Johnny, we are going to fix that leg of yours," and attendants started to administer the anaesthetic. Johnny raised his head and said in a voice that could be heard all over the room, "God bless you, Doctor Dawson, for you have been so good to me." The surgeon looked down at him. Tears came into his eyes. He put his hand on the head of the little fellow and said, "Thank you, Johnny." After the successful operation the surgeon said to the students, "I have operated on many great and prominent men, upon millionaires, senators, governors and have received many large fees, but what that little boy said was the greatest fee I ever received in my life." Can you imagine romance leaving the life of a man like that? Love people and help them. That will keep life always fresh and interesting.

What Men Miss

As we miss the fascination in people, so do the charm and delight of things escape us in our busyness. John Ruskin, shrewd observer of men's foibles as well as their greatness, once sadly commented, "I am not surprised at what men suffer, but I am surprised at what men miss." A whole world of beauty and fascination is spread about us, but we are blind to much of it, not because of any fundamental lack of the quality of appreciation within ourselves, but simply because we do not take time to let this beauty affect us.

Consider the pleasure we miss in books, pictures, and music because we do not take time for them. Every night there stretches over us the inimitable and awe-inspiring canopy of the heavens. Sometimes we are caught by it and brought to a stop, especially in a country place, and we see it again with a sense of newness as one who looks upon something once familiar and it becomes fresh again because of long absence. This glory is for our inspiration nightly, but we are too much in a hurry and we by-pass it. Life was meant to be enjoyed. Life was made for man, not man for life. It was never intended that one should beat his life out on a treadmill, losing his very personality in the rattle and roar of an artificial civilization.

If one should come into a beautiful room with fine paintings on the wall, a fireplace ablaze, easy chairs to rest in and beautiful rugs on the floor, he would conclude that the place had been prepared for his pleasure and happiness. Accordingly, as we look about us in this world with its exquisite beauty and obvious delights, we must surely feel it is good and that life itself is good. Let us take time to live and enjoy it all. He who learns to do so is master of the art of living.

Little Girl Before Operation

There is one other thing, however. A wholesome spiritual life is necessary if anyone is to be happy and in the deepest sense live well here in this world. If you are so busy that you leave God and the things of the spirit out of your life, you are missing the best there is in life's brief experience. Some time ago I was having lunch with an outstanding businessman in a club. I had just clipped an interesting story from a newspaper. It was about a little girl who was operated upon in a New England hospital. It was a serious case. The paper said that as she went into the operating room she prayed out loud a little prayer:

> "Jesus, tender Shepherd, hear me,
>   Bless thy little lamb tonight;
> Through the darkness be thou near me;
>   Keep me safe till morning light."

Then with a trusting smile she said: "I am ready. I am not afraid, for Jesus will take care of me." And, sure enough, He did.

I showed this to my businessman friend. He read it slowly and laid it down with a sort of wistfully pathetic smile. Presently he said after a long silence: "You know something? I once felt like that. The little girl has something that I fear I have let get away from me. I have been too busy, I guess." Then he added slowly, "I have problems too, and I've got to admit sometimes life frightens me a bit. I need a faith like that of the little girl." So do we all, and we can have it if we take time for it.

Four

HOW TO HAVE PEACE OF MIND

In the newspaper I read of a man in London whose sight had just been restored. Having been blind from the age of two years, he, of course, had not remembered how the world and his fellow men appeared and in his blindness had formed some very curious notions, one of which was that most people were tall and slender and that the few who were fat were shaped like bottles. The most striking notion he had formed in his years of sightlessness, however, was that, as he said, "I believed all human faces looked peaceful." Surely, what the blind man felt in his ignorance should be so. It is reasonable to believe that human faces were meant by the good God to look peaceful.

One of the most greatly to be desired boons of this life is peace of mind. Who would not like to have complete peace of mind or at least an approximation of it? It is more to be desired than fine gold or precious jewels or negotiable securities, for if one possesses everything else and does not have peace of mind, what does it get him? Among my acquaintances is an elderly retired minister of the gospel upon whom sits the brooding spirit of wisdom. I called to see him one day, and as he sat in his great chair like some noble old patriarch he took my hand in his thin and emaciated one. His hair was as white as the driven snow; his face, benign and kindly; his eyes, though aged, still lustrous. He said—and I shall never forget it—"My boy, I do not pray that you shall have what the world calls success. I do not pray that you shall have worldly possessions, but I do pray that you shall have peace in your mind and heart." So saying, he lifted up his hands in an ancient benediction, his words falling softly and tenderly, "The Lord bless thee and keep thee; the Lord make his face to shine upon thee and be gracious unto thee; the Lord lift up his countenance upon thee and give thee peace." The impression was unforgettable.

No person in the long journey through life escapes the craving for peace and rest. So declared a distinguished journalist. Active as man may be, eager to press forward in some vital quest, ambitious as he may be for honor or for wealth or for other material rewards, there comes a moment when he would abandon all, if he might, just for a time of utter rest. If we could see into the secret thoughts of great men, if we could lift aside the curtain of their lives and find that which is gripping their minds, we should find often enough the heart-straining wish for peace and rest. Men and women work, strive, aspire and achieve, and take pride in these things. They gain riches, position, influence, friends; are flattered and applauded for what they do if fortune favors them.

But to every such one there comes a time when he pauses for a moment and yields, in his mind, to the temptation to throw everything overboard, to seek out a house in the hills or a cottage by the sea or a hut in some secluded valley and there to escape utterly from the crowding, pushing, choking mass of affairs which hurries him on through the pathways of life.

Dream of Peace

Men fighting their way forward, men standing on the dizzy heights of fame, men struggling to get a foothold and be secure—all have their time of dreaming; and the dreams are dreams of peace, dreams of the silent places, dreams of softly splashing water down green slopes, dreams of the soft murmur of the sea slapping gently on soft shores of sand, dreams of light whispers amid tall and ancient pine trees, dreams of old grape-arbors by a back door, dreams of bending fruit trees in the sweet haze of an Indian summer, dreams of some dim attic and the fragrance of dusty trunks, dreams of haylofts, warm beneath a sloping roof; dreams of green meadows dotted with golden cowslips, dreams of the soft patter of raindrops upon the roof, dreams of daisies nodding in rhythm to the pulse of summer—dreams of peace and rest, all of them.

Faith Gives Peace

It is this that faith does for men. Among its many gifts to humanity is the bestowal of peace. Even the presence of a church has this effect upon us, for there is that in the spire of a church which mutely points away from the stress and struggle of the crowds, reminding us of a central calm above and within. There is that in the sound of a church bell on a Sunday morning which is a reasssuring note to the voyager in life's storms. There is that in the portal of a church which speaks of peace, telling man that when he steps over that threshold, he is in a sanctuary of rest, a quiet place apart where the world with its cares is excluded. There is that in the soft, swinging notes of the great organ which speaks in the tones of everlasting rest. There is that in the message of forgiveness written down in the Book and preached from the pulpit and the reassurance of God's watchful care spoken in faith that causes confidence and calmness to settle upon man's spirit.

One crystal Sunday morning I found myself in the glorious cathedral in Milan, Italy. Surely, there is nothing in all cathedral architecture which surpasses it in exquisite workmanship and in grandeur of conception. As I beheld its great pillars, carrying lofty arches, its massive walls, rising to a noble vaulted roof which retreated into the mystery of shadows, there came to mind the stately words in which Emerson speaks of "the old gray temples of faith and prayer, mountains of stone uplifted by human love and hope, which nature had adopted into the race and given an equal date with Andes and Ararat."

I rented a stool from an attendant and leaned back against one of the great pillars and gave myself over to thought and prayer. The golden, mellow Italian sunshine was pouring through the exquisite windows, catching up their rich color and falling in glory upon the old stones of the cathedral, worn smooth by the tramping feet of many pilgrims through the years.

A shaft of light falling between two pillars revealed a little and very old woman sitting in prayer. She was clad in a simple black dress with a hood of corresponding hue. Her hands, clasping a prayer book, were rough with labor and toil. She was bent in an attitude of devotion while the music from the great organ resounded through the church. She looked up finally and I saw her face, seamed and wrinkled with age but bearing upon it that indescribable sense of peace which showed that there she had found what was promised by Him who in the long ago said: "Peace I give unto you: not as the world giveth, give I unto you. Let not your heart be troubled."

The Era of Stress

We live in a time of intensified stress and strain and it is manifesting itself physically. This is the era of heart disease, high blood pressure, and nervous breakdowns. These afflictions frequently have their

origin largely in hectic and frantic minds rather than
in physical causes. William Muldoon, the famous
athletic trainer, once said, "Men do not die of disease
but of internal combustion." Lack of a peaceful mind
also affects poise, making one irritable and creating
friction between himself and his associates. It distorts
his judgments, dissipates his creative powers, and sub-
tracts from the meaning of living. Where there is no
peace there surely can be no joy and certainly reduced creative activity.

Where, then, is peace of mind to be found? In
nature? Surely this beautiful world is designed to give
man peace. Let him go to the mountains, far removed
from the confusion of the cities, where the great hills,
shrouded in their ever-present mystic haze of blue,
shoulder out the sky. Let him climb into the high
uplands, where the air is crisp and laden with the
exhilarating odor of pine, where the whispering winds
make music through great trees, where the deep val-
leys stretch in pensive quietness between the hills,
rock-ribbed and ancient as the sun. There man can
drink in, if he will, the peace of God. Let the man
seeking peace of mind linger by the sea, watching
its curling foamy breakers surge and fall upon the
beach of clean white sand. Through uncounted centuries the breakers have thus been falling. The roar
through all ages has never ceased. It is as if to say,
"There is plenty of time; there is no hurry; wait;
your own will come to you."

Let one watch the sunlight falling gently upon the

green grass or sifting down onto the black loam of a
forest floor in the stillness of a summer afternoon, or
behold the silvery light of the moon on a white sandy
road or shimmering across water on a starlit night.
Let him feel the soft rain falling against his cheek
on an April day. Let him warm his bones before a
wood fire on a winter night or lift up his eyes to the
stars in a country place where no man-made light
hampers his vision of the fabulous canopy of the
heavens.

All of these surpassingly beautiful things, so beautiful that they bring a choke to the throat, were placed
in the world by God to give man peace but, strangely enough— and sadly enough—one can see all of these
things, love them poignantly and yet not truly find
peace. And why? Obviously, for the reason that peace
of mind is to be found only in your own mind. It
cannot be found elsewhere. If the mind is not at
peace, there can be no peace.

Keep Your Thoughts on God

In a Book which was written by men who knew
all about human beings is a statement by one of the
greatest of them, Isaiah. He learned well the secret
of peace. He writes it in the indelible ink of human
experience—"Thou wilt keep him in perfect peace
whose mind is stayed on thee." He had often suffered
a troubled mind himself, but had discovered that if
he kept his mind on God, he would, in turn be kept

in perfect peace. Is that really true or merely the expression of a wishful desire?

We find, first of all, that one whose mind is stayed on God will come to possess presently something that reflects the imperturbability of God. Sir William Osler once advised all young doctors to be unperturbed at all costs, for how can a doctor who becomes nervous and excited properly handle a case? The advice is good for us all. We cannot meet our problems successfully unless we have a calm and undisturbed spirit. And what is it that with so many of us destroys peace of mind? Isn't it often the annoyances of every day? People admirably meet the big troubles of life. Sorrow, tragedy, disappointment and all major difficulties strike them and some deep inner strength comes to their assistance. They are unbroken by the great storms but the petty annoyances and irritations of daily life will often utterly undermine them. John Burroughs made a wise decision: "One resolution I have made and try always to keep is this—to rise above little things." But it is not easy.

I know a man who, in the business world, is a strong, resourceful leader. He meets the problems of a huge commercial enterprise with imperturbable poise. His wife tells me, however, with some asperity, that if the eggs aren't cooked quite to his liking and the coffee is less than hot or if the morning paper fails to show, he may fly to pieces and depart for the day with the domestic scene one of considerable turmoil. We allow little annoyances, little criticisms, little gossips, little disturbances to destroy our poise and make life miserable. But the person whose mind is stayed on God is kept in perfect peace because his mind rises above insignificant matters.

Faith Removes Fear

Another reason we find perfect peace by keeping our mind on God is that in a remarkable way faith in Him, in His goodness and His constant care, removes fear from us. I have a distinct memory out of the past. It was when I was a very little boy. Walking through crowded city streets with confusion and clamorous noise all about, with hundreds of people passing whom I did not know, I became frightened. Then I recall putting my hand in my father's hand and looking up into his face. He smiled down at me reassuringly and I was no longer afraid. I knew everything would be all right, for my father was big and strong and he loved me, and that was enough. The situation fundamentally is no different when we become adults and find ourselves in the midst of a dark and confused world. Put your hand in the hand of the Father. Look up and by the long vision of faith see His smile. He is big and strong and He loves you and will take care of you.

Don't Be Afraid, You Have a Friend

The person who learns to keep his mind stayed

on God also has that factor essential to peace of
mind, a friend to whom he may unreservedly open
up his heart. There is in us all a deep-seated necessity which requires the opportunity to freely pour out
our inmost hearts upon occasion. It is of unquestion-
able value to talk over the deep matters of one's
life with another and understanding person. It makes
problems seem clearer than merely to reflect upon
them within one's own mind. Themistocles told us
that "speech is like the cloth of Arras, opened and
spread abroad whereby the imagery doth appear;
whereas in thought it lies but as in packs."

When we take out our burdens and problems and
lay them open for a sympathetic friend to examine
with us, their outline and form and imagery appear
more clearly to ourselves and the confusing things
which disturb us are lost in a sense of new-found
understanding and peace.

As students, we were advised by our wise professor
that the study of philosophy would be clearer to us
if we talked it over among ourselves instead of trying
to think it through individually. This we did, and
while doubtless our conversations were far from il-
luminating philosophically, this practice at least
helped us to orient our own problems. There are
some things, however, in which even a trusted human
friend cannot be a satisfactory repository for our con-
fidences. In such cases men discover that only God
can satisfy their need. It is for this reason that some
old men and old women, like those painted by Rem-

brandt, have on their faces an ineffable peace. For long years they had known that by keeping their minds on God as the intimate companion of their life journey they entered into an inner quietness and confidence.

She Did All the Talking

A woman came to my study one day who obviously was not one of the devout members of the flock. She swept in impetuously, trailed by the confused aroma of perfume, tobacco and liquor. She was considerably decorated facially. With a jaunty, even flippant manner, she said: "Imagine me in the study of a minister! My friends would all laugh if they could see me here." I did not say so, but the thought crossed my mind that my friends, too, might laugh if they could see her there.

She inquired in a businesslike manner how much time I had at my disposal, to which I replied, "Thirty minutes." Shen then outlined the interview by saying that she would tell me what her troubles were and that when she had finished, I would diagnose and prescribe. She explained that she had had no contact with the Church since girlhood, but that now under the stress of great trouble she felt that a minister perhaps could help her. She had conversed, she said, with one or two close friends but had gained no satisfaction.

She proceeded therewith to talk in a steady stream

for thirty minutes. Then with a glance at the clock and a mumbled apology she arose, saying her time was up and she must go. I noticed that the sense of strain and nervousness which had characterized her when she entered the room seemed to have departed, and with a most attractive smile she put out her hand and said brightly: "Thank you so much. You have helped me a great deal"—and was gone. She left me scratching my head and asking myself what I had done for her, for I had scarcely been able to get a word in edgewise.

Then it occurred to me that she did not want advice or need it, that she did not require to have her case diagnosed or a prescription given, but that what she needed was a sympathetic listener, whom she could trust and to whose shoulders she could shift her own load. She departed, having in a sense rested her burdens upon one whom she considered a representative of God and by that means upon God Himself. This woman was following as best she could an instinctive realization that only from God could she find a sense of unity for her distracted mind. I wished afterward I might have been quick enough to tell her that if she would keep her mind on God, she would never again find herself so deeply in confusion.

Unclean Wounds Slow to Heal

Still another thing must be said too. Men are troubled by distressed minds devoid of peace, because

of the wrong they do. It is almost impossible to carry
around in one's mind a sense of guilt and have mental
peace. Men in a moment of weakness do something
wrong and they ever afterward may be fundamentally
unhappy because of the persistent memory of an un-
forgiven misdeed. A sin in the mind acts much like
a wound in the body. A clean wound will heal quickly and completely but an unclean wound will not
heal quickly, or for that matter at all until it is
cleansed. Sorrow is a clean wound. It hurts terribly,
and the cut may be deep, but there is no infection
in it and nature binds it up. Sin is an unclean wound.
It too cuts deeply.

Santayana in *The Last Puritan* tells us that the man
who gives a wrong twist to your mind meddles with
you just as surely as a man who hits you in the eye.
The hurt is not so sharp but the effect is longer lasting. Sin, having wounded you, sets up an infection
which unless eliminated from your mind will poison
your entire life. It will reach the nerves and make them
jumpy. It will affect the heart and accelerate its action. It will penetrate to the stomach and upset your
digestion. It will get into your organs of taste and
take away the pleasure of your food. It will haunt
your mind and disturb your sleep—in short, it will
completely deprive you of peace. There is only one
cure for it.

A man came to see me. He was of evident culture
and, I take it, of wealth and social standing in his
community. He said he had come to New York to

consummate a business deal, the most important of his career. He told me that for some time he had found it difficult to consolidate his powers of concentration and that now when he needed them most, he found himself peculiarly ineffective. He complained of growing nervousness and unhappiness. He said that he had attempted to pray, but that his prayers seemed ineffectual and that he could not feel near to God. He informed me that in his desperation he had attended our church, and knowing no one else to whom he might turn had sought my counsel as a clergyman.

I have had at times a peculiar sense that at such an interview the two of us were not alone, that a third Person was present, guiding and directing the conversation. I had such an impression on this occasion, for inadvertently I acted with a wisdom which I would not otherwise have enjoyed. We discussed many things in an attempt to ferret out the thing that was disturbing him. Obviously, it was something deep in his mind. In this case it did not have to be drawn up from subconscious depths, but it was a deep wound.

I said to him quietly, "Have you done anything morally wrong?" He flushed and was embarrassed but finally said, "Yes, I have." I asked him to tell me about it. He replied that he had never told anybody about it. I counseled, "Perhaps that is the block impeding the flow of normal power through your mind." He started to talk; haltingly, hesitatingly at first, but as he began to unload, he spoke with a torrential rush of words. It became a catharsis of the mind, full and complete, and the old, dark, evil things gushed out of a mind where they had become congealed, effectively checking the passage of personal power. When he had completed his story and the last word had died away, there appeared on his face a look of deep relief, and brisk, incisive, decisive person that he was, he said: "You have found it. That is the solution of the matter."

Of course I had suggested that he dedicate himself to God, ask and receive forgiveness, and as he departed it was evident that he was a new man. Since then he has not forgotten the secret but has kept his mind fixed on God and God's way of living and has never forgotten that God saved him from a broken life. He now has peace, and I do not believe he will ever lose it.

Five

THE DISCOVERY OF HAPPINESS

If you could have the thing you most desire; if you could realize your dearest wish, for what would you ask? What is the highest personal good beside which all other values become secondary in importance? Many people, perhaps most people, would answer in terms of financial security, health, power, love, or the realization of some ambition or desire cherished at the moment. In each case the answer would of necessity be partial.

Would not the wise man, if his reply be thoughtful and reflective, conclude that the one great thing most to be desired in this fleeting life is that state or quality we call happiness? This is the basic motive underlying all our work and struggle. Man's activity, in a strict sense, is motivated by no single objective. He is driven quite largely by necessity, and varying impulses feed the stream of his purpose, but reduced to its simplest terms, so far as that is possible, the desire

81

for happiness indubitably is the fundamental goal of every individual.

Happiness is to be distinguished from pleasure. Pleasure differs from happiness less in form than in quality. Happiness is a concept involving something deeper, richer, more satisfying, more spiritual, and therefore longer lasting than pleasure. The essential difference between the two terms is illustrated by the fact that one could, for example, achieve real and abiding happiness by dying for another person, whereas such an act of self-sacrifice could by no means be described as pleasure. In *A Tale of Two Cities* Dickens tells us that they said of Sydney Carton, who gave his life for one he loved, his was "the peacefulest face in Paris that night." Carton manifestly had experienced happiness rather than pleasure.

Happiness the Chief Desire

Happiness thus conceived is the supreme desire. Some may object to this conclusion on the ground that it places a low estimate on life's objectives; that the ultimate purpose of living is to find God or truth or beauty, to develop goodness or, as Carlyle would have it, to achieve excellence in work. Is it not true, however, that in the long run these boons are of value for the reason that they in themselves bring us happiness? We seek God because our souls tell us the truth which experience confirms—that to find God is to find true happiness. It is, therefore, sound to say that the chief end of man is to know God, for to enjoy Him forever is to possess the quality known as happiness. The case for happiness as the chief good seems to be on solid footing.

As we observe people today, it is evident that many are not happy. People have their jokes and try to act released but with tragic frequency their gaiety is simulated. Underneath they are oppressed by what Wordsworth termed with sharp discernment "the weary weight of this unintelligible world." People go to movies and laugh at comedy if it is funny— which quite often it is not, for vulgarity in any form lacks the subtlety of humor, and their laughter is less than hearty. It is often on the surface and the glisten of tears is ill concealed. There is a profound undercurrent of sadness which has robbed life of much of its oldtime spontaneity, and spontaneous joy is essential to happiness. As Santayana tells us in *The Last Puritan*—"To be happy was to sing; not to be made to sing, or to sing by rote, or as an art or for a purpose, but spontaneously, religiously, because something sang within you and all else for the moment was remote and still."

It is to be expected, of course, that existing conditions in a world of racial tension, economic trouble, uneasy peace and international insecurity should not be conducive to happiness, but the trouble is a deeper one. Long ago Clutton-Brock, the distinguished essayist, was saying, "In spite of our games and our science and machinery, we find ourselves growing duller." The

plain fact of the matter is that our age has for years
been losing contact with the deep springs of human
happiness and we shall not again enjoy life in the
profoundest sense until we re-establish that contact.

We fell into the old and subtle error of thinking
that contentment is dependent upon things. As we
piled up our gold and beheld the appliances and gad-
gets which a prolific science heaped in amazing pro-
fuseness upon us, we became convinced beyond any
possibility of error that the golden age of happiness
had come at long last. The world was now so full of
a number of things we should all be as happy as
kings, or so we imagined.

The Lost Happiness

But as the child only a few days after Christmas
wearies of his toys, so men and women everywhere
began to cast around for the old delight in life which
had escaped them amidst the glitter of their new possessions. Perhaps we are now beginning to realize
that we have been very adolescent in our conceited
notion that in our generation reposes the wisdom of
the ages. From the shades of a remote past comes
the voice of Marcus Aurelius, "Remember that very
little is needed to make a happy life." But we smile;
we know better than that. We confuse the ability to
make fast cars to quickly get us to places we have
no desire to go, and television to bring us programs,

many of which are scarcely worth viewing, with genuine progress in the art of living.

Progress, as we shall discover, depends not upon speed but upon peace, not upon noise but upon quietness. If our many inventions can free man from drudgery and provide him with leisure for cultural and spiritual advancement, they will exercise the salutary function for which they surely were ordained; otherwise, they will drive us quite mad. There are happy evidences now that we are learning discrimination regarding the intrinsic value of things as we become increasingly aware that our naïve dependence upon them for happiness is not warranted.

Our generation is not happy, moreover, because it is increasingly an age of sensation. Sensation is soon exhausted, and, like a cumulative drug, requires heavier doses until finally the very power to respond to stimulation is satiated. We are greatly interested in diet as it affects the body, all of which is not without value, but multitudes of us feed upon a mental and cultural froth which is producing in society a general condition of spiritual sclerosis. Plainly, we are undernourished spiritually, as is shown by the discontent, weariness, and false stimulation of life everywhere. Consider the vast number of suicides. They totaled, I am informed, nearly eight per cent of the death claims of one large insurance company in a recent year. These were people who could stand the thinness of life no longer and in desperation flung themselves out of it.

It is reminiscent of a terrible line in the Scriptures: "He gave them their desires but sent leanness into their souls."

Happiness is to be found in sources deeper than man-made things. Lawrence of Arabia, in his *Seven Pillars of Wisdom,* relates a curious incident which reveals man's hunger for something more fundamental than that represented by his own design and craftsmanship. With an Arab friend he rode far out on the desert to the ruins of an ancient palace which, according to tradition, had been erected by a Roman ruler for his queen. Legend has it that the mortar was kneaded not with water but with the essential oil of flowers. In each room the odor was different.

The Arab led Lawrence about, explaining that this was the rose room, this the jasmine room, that the violet room, and they sniffed the atmosphere for the lingering scent of those flowers. At length the Arab said, "But come, smell the best odor of all," and taking him to a broken casement they smelled the clean air off the desert. It had come long and lazily over hundreds of miles from the far-away Euphrates, over vast expanses of desert where little human habitation is found. Lovingly, it had whispered among the grasses and played with the sands until it possessed within itself the essence of the good earth, the mother of all mankind.

Deeply the two men smelled, drinking in that mystic affinity which man feels for the dust from whence he came and to which at last he shall return. In its often frustrated search for happiness mankind must turn finally to those fair winds that blow from the land of the spirit where the whir of motors is lost in an ancient stillness. There life in its natural quality recovers its rightful dominance over life that is artificial and litter-filled. Then long-unused springs of human happiness will flow freely once more.

Sources of Happiness

Considering the sources of happiness, it would perhaps be well to touch upon those which are commonly considered essential to the joy of life. Some people think that if they could have money, they would be happy. Money does make its contribution to happiness, and it is foolish to deny that fact. The moralist may declare that the love of money is the root of all evil, and it is well enough to refer slightingly to it as "filthy lucre," but most of us like the root just the same, and the unsanitary condition of the currency will not deter us from gladly accepting it.

Money can help give happiness by relieving one from common financial worries. It mightily helps in contentment to be in a position to pay the rent regularly and to settle for your life insurance. But money is no guarantee of happiness, for have we not all seen rich people who are unhappy and poor people who are very happy? It is significant, as Chesterton reminds

us in his study of Charles Dickens, that simple gladness and optimism are frequently found most completely among the poor rather than the affluent.

We might also reasonably expect to look for happiness in bodily health. Surely, health is a great blessing,
and fortunate indeed is the individual who has it, but
not every healthy person is happy nor does health
insure happiness. I recall once having a very severe
toothache, sitting in a dentist's office awaiting my turn.
As I sat there, suffering as only a toothache can tor-
ture, I looked enviously out of the window at the
people passing by.

Disconsolately, I meditated, wondering how many
in that passing throng had toothaches, and I decided
that the happy ones were those who did not have
toothaches and that the unhappy ones were those who,
like myself, did have an aching tooth. I came to the
conclusion that if only I could stop that tooth from
aching, I would never be unhappy again, the fallacy
of which reasoning later became quite apparent. There
are healthy people who are not happy and, on the
other hand, there are invalids whose faces indicate a
spirit that has overcome the world and realized the
secret of happiness.

Why the Cow Is Happy

There are those who feel that they would be perfectly happy if they could be relieved of all cares and
responsibilities. They would be everlastingly content,

they argue, if they could see the last of all the common perplexities and problems of this life. Dr. William Lyon Phelps answered that idea by philosophizing that in such a case the happiest being on earth would be neither man nor woman but the American cow. He suggested the American cow because in other countries cows are hitched up and made to draw loads, whereas in this land of freedom they are cows of leisure.

In a whimsical page or so Professor Phelps deliciously pursues his quaint thesis: "The cow," he says, "completes her toilet for the day with one flick of her tail. This is a distinct advantage over humanity, for the average woman requires forty-five minutes at least and a man little less." The cow does not even worry about her meals but just peacefully munches the lush grass, after which she reclines in the shade of a tree until time for the next meal. There is upon her placid features no pale cast of thought. She does not find it necessary to worry her mind about anything. She need not be concerned about a salary reduction, or who is going to be elected President or about saving the Constitution. She does not have to meet a payroll or preach a sermon or find a job or write a book.

There is no apprehensiveness on the face of a cow. She is a perfect humanist in that the world is what it is and she can do nothing about it, so why worry about it? But with due consideration for all the benefits of such placidity of life, who, queries Doctor Phelps, would want to be a cow? For most of us life

with all its cares, problems and strivings is a decided
advantage over bovine peace. William James found
a famous religious retreat center too idealistically perfect for him. He preferred the imperfect but far more
interesting world of labor and struggle.

How to Be Happy

What are some positive suggestions for those who
are sincerely looking for the chance to be happy? First
of all, I believe it will be found in the simple things
familiarly about us. Look for it in a city street bustling
with traffic, across which the sunlight falls in late
afternoon, making it as mellow as an old master. Get
the delight of discovering a fugitive little park tucked
away in an old backwater of a city's life, to which
clings the atmosphere of romantic days long gone.
Find it in the vision of a ship's funnel at a street's
end, bringing to one the romantic suggestion of dreamy,
far-away ports.

Look for your happiness not in that shining metal
which corrodes, but in the smell of newly turned soil;
in rain against a windowpane, running down in mean-
dering rivulets; in sunlight on a summer's afternoon,
splashing down through the leaves to a well-kept lawn,
or in the lazy sun-speckled bank of a trout stream.
Look for it in an autumn landscape with blue haze
over the hills and the haunting, fugitive sadness of
dying year. Rustle your way among falling leaves on
an autumn afternoon or feel the crunch of snow under-

foot on a starlit winter night. Warm yourself before
the ruddy glow of a wood fire, stretching out your
legs in glad content. These are the things that make
a man so happy inside of him that he could sing
aloud. These are fundamental things, old and deep.

Love to Live

Once on a Sunday morning a little old lady with a
"face with gladness overspread" came up to shake
hands. I asked routinely, "How are you this morning?"
knowing full well the question to be superfluous.
"Oh," she replied, "I'm always all right," and added,
"I love to live," which sentence in its simple eloquence
was a sermon in itself. She added, "This little poem
is just the way I feel about it," and pressing it into my
hand she went off, leaving a trail of sunshine in her
wake. This appealing verse by Grace Crowell is what
she gave me as part of her philosophy of happiness:

> "I have found such joy in simple things:
>   A plain, clean room, a nut-brown loaf of bread,
> A cup of milk, a kettle as it sings,
>   The shelter of a roof above my head,
> And in a leaf-faced square upon a floor
> Where yellow sunlight glimmers through a door.
>
> "I have found such joy in things that fill
>   My quiet days: a curtain's blowing grace,
> A growing plant upon a window sill,
>   A rose, fresh-cut and placed within a vase;
> A table cleared, a lamp beside a chair,
> And books I long have loved beside me there.

"Oh, I have found such joy I wish I might
   Tell every woman who goes seeking far
For some elusive, feverish delight,
   That very close to home the great joys are:
These fundamental things—old as the race,
Yet never, through the ages, commonplace." [1]

There is another simple thing that helps one to be happy and enjoy life. All of these things are simple, but do not underestimate them because of that fact, for simplicity is usually the special repository of the greatest truths. The profound and the simple are first cousins. The great secret is that happiness is not to be found in getting but in giving. It is not what you do for yourself that will give you the greatest happiness but, rather, what you do for others. You can prove this to yourself by noticing that warm glow which comes when you do a kindly act. That is why the Great Thinker, Jesus, who talked much about these things, said, "It is more blessed to give than to receive."

As you read these words, if you are unhappy, think of the most unfortunate person you know. At the first opportunity go to him and help him in some way, even if only by a friendly word. Just telephone and say, "I was just thinking about you and decided to give you a call."

It may surprise him but it will make him happy.

[1] "I Have Found Such Joy," from *Light of the Years,* by Grace Noll Crowell. Reprinted by permission of Harper & Brothers, publishers.

However, I am thinking of what it will do to you. It will set little songs singing in your heart. There is no joy like it, and it will make the whole world brighter for you. More than that, in this matter of giving for others there is a priceless secret of personal power. Lloyd Douglas graphically portrayed what I mean in his books, *Forgive Us Our Trespasses* and *The Magnificent Obsession*. His thesis and mine is that when one freely gives to others without thought of gain for himself and with a sincere purpose, he sets free in his own personality a power which endows life with a richness hitherto undreamed of.

This was what Jesus was always trying to get people to do. Many Christians fail at this point, and their lives are like a twenty-five-watt bulb when they could shine with the brilliance of one hundred and fifty watts. Or, to use another figure, many people, even members of the church in good standing, are like one rowing a boat with great labor when all the time under the seat is a motor which, without toil, could send the craft forward at great speed. This power which lifts the individual is releasable by the simple practice of forgetting oneself and devoting activities and thought to assisting others.

When Things Went Stale

A distinguished editorial writer told me that for years he lived the selfish life, making money only to give himself everything he wanted. At length an over-

whelming ennui overtook him, drabness set in. Things
lost piquancy and became dreary. Love died between
his wife and himself and they were divorced.

Then it happened that he fell upon a strange secret.
He learned that the Great Teacher was right when
long ago He said, "He that saveth his life shall lose
it, but he that giveth his life shall find it an hundred-
fold." This man truly had lost life, for little remains
when happiness is gone. He was saving his life and
he had lost it, but now he began to give it away,
and, wonder of wonders, he had it all back again,
only this time much deeper and richer than ever before. And even as he told me his story he took pains
to make it clear that he was not a churchman or even
a Christian in the formal sense. I assured him that
had nothing to do with it, that quite apart from labels
of any sort he had through his self-giving released the
power of Christ in his personality.

With a smile he said: "Perhaps I have been converted. Yes," he reflected, using the great old word
gingerly, "perhaps I have been converted." Indeed,
and what is it but conversion when a man who was
dead is now alive? Something deep within the man
bubbled up in a buoyant gladness which made one
know that for him life now is good. People are so
foolish in living a fractional life when it could easily
be complete. The mistake is in allowing thought and
activity to focus inwardly. In so doing we become
abnormally conscious of ourselves, to the end that we
develop envy, greed, touchiness, self-pride—all misery-

making characteristics. In a word, the self becomes horribly conscious of self because it is concerned only with self.

On the contrary, when one begins to focus himself outwardly, he forgets himself and the many irritating factors which formerly troubled him. Even the small and pesky cares scamper like shadows before the rising sun or they become so innocuous that they are easily handled. They love their commanding influence. The outgoing life is the normal life, the well-adjusted life, and only in such inner unity of personality as the self-giving process engenders can happiness exist.

Clean Life Up to Be Happy

There is still another suggestion that must be made in any adequate treatment of the problem of human happiness. To find real and unalloyed happiness it is necessary to live a clean, upright life and to enjoy the peace of an approving conscience. Psychology gives this principle honored place in its understanding of human personality. The new terminology does not conceal the identity of the old yet ever new truth that "the wages of sin is death."

Mr. Walter Lippmann, by no means a Sunday-school superintendent of the fundamentalist variety, or, for that matter, any variety, confirms our thesis. "There is now," he said, "a generation approaching middle age which exerted the privilege of attacking the Puritan or Victorian tradition without restraint.

Their convictions are reported in many of the late
works of fiction. Do they report they have found happiness in their freedom? Hardly," continued Mr. Lippmann; "instead of the happiness they were promised,
they have found only the wasteland." It has always
been so and I suppose always will be, that an unspiritual, immoral, pagan life in the last analysis brings unhappiness. No man can live a life that is wrong and be
happy. This is not a rule established by the Church.
Nature wove it into the plan of things long before
there ever was a Church.

As a boy I was sometimes under the care of an
old-school small-town doctor. Before the general use
of motor cars he drove up to the house in a horse-
drawn buggy. I would watch him from the window.
A big man, when he stepped out of his buggy it rocked
like a ship in a storm. From behind the seat he took
out a large stone attached to a strap by means of
which he anchored the horse, a superfluous precaution,
for the nag immediately went to sleep. Carrying his
little black case, the doctor came in like a breath of
fresh air though trailed by familiar medicinal odors.
He sat down by the bed, felt my pulse, pounded my
chest, looked at my tongue, and took my temperature.

He then opened his case and gave me some little
pills—I often suspicioned they were used for every ail-
ment about the countryside, but at any rate I got
well to tell the story. I liked this old country doctor,
and though now his office is closed forever and the
last patient has been treated, I shall never forget him.

Today one doctor diagnoses your case and another operates. One removes your teeth, another your appendix, another your tonsils, and another what is left of you, and doubtless they do it more efficiently than the old doctor. But, even so, I, for one, rise up to pay him tribute.

Cure for Stomach Ache

Once when he came to see me about a stomach ache of which I complained, after prescribing for it, he put his great, kindly hand upon my head and tousled it, saying: "Pains in the body will heal, sonny, but never do anything that will give you a pain in the mind. I cannot heal that kind." But, he added, "There is a Great Physician who can, but I hope you will not need Him for that."

He would not have called himself a psychiatrist, that would have been rather newfangled for him, but in a deep sense he was just that. He was a physician of the mind—yes, and of the soul too, for he knew that pains in the mind caused by wrong living take the bloom off life and rob it of happiness. Keep the pains out of the mind by a simple, virtuous life, or, if the pain is already there, go to that greatest of all Physicians, who keeps office in the New Testament, and let Him by faith make you whole again.

Six

THE ESCAPE FROM FEAR

A British publishing house issued, some years ago, a volume of sermons, not by ministers, as might be supposed, but by laymen, under the title, *If I Could Preach Only Once*. One of these sermons was by Gilbert Chesterton. One would expect him to say something clever if not wise. He did. It was both clever and wise. "If I had only one sermon to preach," Chesterton declared, "it would be a sermon against fear."

Why should this eminent man of letters single out so ordinary an adversary? First of all, because fear is the universal nemesis. It is one of man's most common enemies. It touches every one of us in some way. Many people, for example, have financial fears. They range all the way from fears about one's business to the loss of a job. We have fears of ill health, anticipating the direful consequences of being overtaken by some bodily affliction. We allow ourselves to be made miserable by fear of what the future holds or fears of the consequences of past acts and decisions. Fears of one kind and another haunt us and cast a shadow over our happiness.

A second reason for speaking out against fear is its distressingly harmful effects. No person is at his best or in full control of his powers if he is the victim of fear. The effect of fear on an individual is illustrated by its physical reactions which should, in turn, cause us to carefully reflect upon its serious spiritual and mental results. My church is so situated at the center of New York's busy life that many couples come to us to be married. Most of them I do not know personally, so that I can recount the following incident without embarrassing those involved. This couple stood before the altar and I observed that the groom was exceedingly nervous. His fears were all but destroying his power of co-ordination, nor could I assign any real reason for it. The bride certainly was a mild and harmless-appearing lady.

Frightened Bridegroom

In the ceremony the groom is required to say, "With this ring I thee wed and with my worldly goods I thee endow." This bridegroom, his tongue incapacitated by fear, said instead, "With this ring I thee wed and with thy worldly goods I *me* endow." Whether this represented some covert acquisitive instinct I have no way of knowing, but when he sought to place the ring on the bride's finger, fear had so destroyed his muscular control that he could not place it where it belonged and the bride, with a masterful gesture of self-assertiveness, took the ring from his trembling and clammy hand and herself placed it firmly on her own finger.

This simple illustration is sufficient to show how fear destroys one's physical efficiency. In many other ways fear lays its paralyzing hand upon an individual and becomes a chief obstacle to the full development of personality and to the achievement of success in life. The person who wishes to become adept in the art of living must learn to conquer and subdue his fears.

This is a problem common to us all, and I want to state at the outset the encouraging fact that any individual can escape from fear. Remember this, however—only *you* can conquer your fears. I can write about them and I can conquer my own fears, but neither I nor anyone else can conquer your fears for you. Others may help you but ultimately you must do it yourself. I want to help you by asking you now while you are reading these words to lay your fears out before you and see them not as you imagine them to be but as they are.

The first step and, for that matter, a large part of the campaign against one's fears is to get a complete and thorough-going knowledge of them—again I say, not as they seem to be but as they really are. The reason fears are apparently so difficult to defeat is because we allow them to remain vague and shadowy. Like any object in the semidarkness, they assume

grotesque shapes and appear larger in size and therefore more formidable than they actually are. Bring
them out into the light of day and watch them shrivel
up.

A fear is not unlike a ghost. It frightens you in the
gloom, but there isn't much to it when you get it
into the light. Most of the things one fears never
happen; at least they do not amount to anything. As
one frog in a pond may sound like a hundred when
one is trying to sleep, so one little fact may be enlarged by mental fear and distorted imagining out of
all proportion to its real size.

North Woods Drama

Once in a lonely cabin on a dark night, deep in
the North Woods, I heard on the porch noises that
sent a shiver up my spine. It sounded like the cautious approach of several intruders. I sat transfixed,
rooted to my chair, with every hair seemingly standing on end. Newspaper accounts of a recent murder
in that section flashed across my mind. This is the
end, I thought, but I was far from being prepared to
die. I didn't want to die; I wanted to get out of
there. Finally, unable to stand the suspense longer
and desperation lending bravado, I leaped to the door
and flung it open, expecting to see a whole array
of gangsters with machine guns and pistols. Instead,
a little chipmunk scurried off into the darkness, leaving
me limp and mortified but yet the learner of a great

lesson, namely, that it is very salutary to get a good look at your fears, and that when you do, they are much less impressive than you had imagined them to be.

Fear is also eliminated, not by an act of will but by a magnificent displacement in which some large purpose or interest crowds it out. It is difficult to achieve the conquest of fear by simply saying, "I will throw fear out of my mind." That often serves only to make it all the more stubborn. A direct frontal attack is not always, indeed seldom, the best strategy. A better plan is to let something big come into your thinking, something that will fire your imagination, capture your interest, and be so tremendously significant that there shall remain no room for fears or worries in your mind. Displacement rather than operation has proven to be the most successful method for dealing with fear.

Dawn at Sea

One night, crossing the ocean, I was unable to sleep because of worries and anxieties. Before dawn I arose and went up to the hurricane deck, where I was entirely alone. It was neither dark nor light. A murky gray pallor hung over ship and sea. The black smoke from the funnels drifting sluggishly off to the east blended smuttily into the gloomy atmosphere. The ship, lifting on a gentle swell, pushed forward heavily through the murk. Shadows were everywhere.

The entire dreary scene was but a reflection of my own inner mood for I was the harried victim of worry and fear. Then on the eastern horizon came a faint glow. I watched it rise higher in the sky. It was for all the world like a mammoth chimney with an enormous glowing, ruddy fire on the hearth. Presently the far-off sky became a delicate rose color, which spread, as I watched, to the tip of every wave. The sun pushed his shining orb high above the horizon and bathed the ship and sea and sky in golden, glorious sunshine. The Ancient Mariner once saw the same sublime spectacle:

> "The sun came up upon the left,
> Out of the sea came he,
> And he shone bright . . ."

Then I saw something never to be forgotten. It seemed that of a sudden all the shadows that had been lurking in every corner fled from their hiding places, scampered across the deck, for all the world like mice, and leaped into the sea. The ship became in an instant a thing of glistening white beauty, gliding over a sea of blue and gold. It struck me that, of course, I should have known the shadows could not remain in the same place with the sun, for the sun is too big and strong for shadows. It taught me a lesson and it is a great lesson for you too. Let some real big thing take over in your life and all the dark, lurking shadowy fears will scamper away because they have no power in themselves. The process of displacement is the road away from fear.

Another thing which will greatly help in the escape from fear is to establish what we may call a great companionship. When one goes his own way a loner in his own strength alone, fears are bound to creep in and hold their place tenaciously. It is for this reason that it is helpful to go into difficult places two by two. Mutual support in an undertaking gives added courage to each individual involved. In a strange and remarkable way the touch of a human hand, the feel of a shoulder alongside our own, and the sound of a friendly voice give us courage. A faithful companion or comrade adds to fortitude and serves as an antidote to fear.

I Sell Aluminum Ware

Another personal illustration may throw light on the point at hand. When I was a high school student, I undertook the sale of aluminum ware during the vacation period one summer. For fifteen dollars I purchased a complete outfit of aluminum cooking utensils together with a well-written and persuasive sales talk. After mastering the latter I set out alone for a nearby town to begin my sales campaign.

I walked up the street and passed the first house. "They probably don't need any aluminum ware," I reasoned. I by-passed the second house. "It looks as if nobody is at home," I explained to myself. Then I confessed to myself that I was only compromising with my fears and determined to try the third house if it killed me. With uncertain steps I approached the house, climbed the steps with knees shaking and mouth dry. Silently I rehearsed the sales talk and, praying that no one would answer, gingerly pressed the bell.

A large and fearful-looking woman—or at least, so she appeared to my worried eyes—opened the door and with a cold glare barked, "Well, what do you want?" My sales talk completely fled and timidly and apologetically I said, "You don't want any aluminum ware, do you?" "Of course not," she snapped, and slammed the door in my face. I gave up for the day and ignominiously returned home.

That evening I managed to sell half interest in my business to a friend of mine. Together we set out for the same town next morning. We stopped at the street which was the scene of my failure on the previous day. I said to my friend, "We will go to the next street; I worked this one yesterday." He took one side of the street and I, the other. He approached his first house and I approached mine. As he stood ready to ring the bell he looked across at me and waved his hand with a cheery smile as if to say, "Go ahead, old boy, I'm with you."

I responded in kind; rang the bell with high courage; and in a moment the door opened and there stood the smallest woman I ever saw and the least

offensive or, so at least she appeared to my determined gaze, and she was soon signing her name to
the dotted line. I ended up by making a good sale.
What made the difference? Simply the fact that I
now had a friend whose companionship gave me
courage and dissipated my fears and enabled me to
coordinate and apply my own powers.

In this world, things frequently become hard and
difficult and fears gang up on us, but if we have the
Great Companion with us, it helps us tremendously
to overcome all fears. Who is this Great Companion?
Multitudes of happy, courageous, victorious men and
women have found such a friend in Jesus Christ.

There was Samuel Rutherford, who in the dark
days of religious tyranny in Scotland sturdily remarked:
"I have learned in this ill weather to go on the lee
side of Christ. I put Christ in between me and the
storm and, lo, I walk on the sunny side of the brae."
He had learned the reality of companionship with
Christ. This is a simple secret which real and vital
Christians have discovered to be indispensable to their
happiness and well-being.

Of course there are some people who will tell you
that this is all a matter of imagination and therefore
a delusion. That is because to them Christ is not a
real person. They regard Him as only a great character
of history, who lived long ago. Such a restricted view
multitudes of the most discriminating people have
discovered to be inaccurate. They have found Him
tremendously real and very personal. It is curious

that some people should assume a skeptical attitude
toward this fact when we are very ready to believe
the most amazing things in science. Why is it that
we are ready to believe these wonders in the natural
realm? Simply because the general principle involved
in each has been factually demonstrated. By the same
token the fact of Christ has been repeatedly demonstrated with equal scientific accuracy.

Amazing New Life

Here, for example, is a noted dramatist whose life
had taken a tailspin. The charm and excitement of
living had left him. His creative capacity became slug-
gish. He was driven back upon himself and the experience was unsatisfactory.

He had a summer estate on Long Island. He drove
out one evening and went to his room. Something
impelled him to turn to a Book long unused, and on
that quiet summer night he took up the New Testament. As he read the ancient pages he found himself
strangely moved. He read on and on with growing excitement. For many these words seem but cold print,
but as he read they began to glow and sparkle. The
room, so he says, seemed filled with a Presence at
once fascinating and overpowering.

So moved was he that he dropped upon his knees
by the window and looking out saw the moonlight
falling softly upon the lawns. Peace and beauty were
everywhere in the outer world but nothing could

equal the sublime peace that filled his mind. He arose
with the breathtaking conviction that same One who
had walked by Galilee long ago, saying words of peace,
walked that night by the shores of Long Island Sound.
That same Person touched and changed this modern
man. As a result of this experience he recovered zest
and freshness together with renewed creative power.
He subsequently produced some most impressive work.
Yes, the reality of God in Christ is a fact demonstrable
and sure. Upon it we may depend.

There is no prescription for escaping from fear that
will not ultimately lead us to the proposition that the
best way—in fact, the only way—to be sure that your
life is completely rid of fear is to think and live the
Jesus way. Its workability has been proven in personal
experience so often that it can hardly be ignored by
an intelligent person.

Practice Your Religion to End Fear

John Rathbone Oliver, in his famous book entitled
Fear, which I believe is the best thing in popular form
ever written on the subject, said that those who are
the freest from fear are those who believe in and
practice—note the emphasis—*practice* the Christian
religion. A vital, fully convinced Christian saturates
his mind with such truths as "The Lord is my shepherd; I shall not want." He can say, and mean it, "I
will fear no evil for thou art with me. Thy rod and
thy staff, they comfort me." He has learned not to

let his heart be troubled, for he believes in God, and because he believes in God he loves God, and, accordingly, has achieved the great and sublime truth that "perfect love casteth out fear." Anyone who actually lives in the literature and spirit of the New Testament will acquire after a while a quiet confidence that nothing can shake.

A great Japanese, Kagawa, a preacher and social worker, once visited our country. Everyone noted that he carried about himself a sense of peace and poise, an inner strength and confidence that was truly remarkable. Kagawa had discovered a priceless secret, and he gave us his secret by saying that if one will do as he did, "immerse himself over a long period in the grace of God," he will enter into a profound calm that nothing can destroy. Kagawa said that encountering mobs, threatened by soldiers, hurt by opponents, the calm never left him. His eyesight was threatened; disease afflicted him; but he never lost his calm. He testified that he was often amazed by the depth of this peace. This he assured us he found in God through the medium of Jesus Christ. In that relationship he lost his fears.

There are those who in their unwillingness to understand Christ's teachings confuse them with creed, ceremony, repressive ethics, and moribund tradition. That is a very faulty description of Christ's way of living faith. A better picture of it is as a spring of clear, crystal, refreshing water which satisfies every thirst of man, gives him strength, cleanses him from his sins, and washes away all of the dark stains and fears from his life.

Once a radiant, happy, virile Teacher walked this earth. He lived in an ancient day but He is a universal figure, as much at home in our time as in His own. He says to all, "Come unto the waters and drink." Those who have accepted His invitation and have taken the water of life have found a healing property that has cured them of every ill of mind and soul, including fear, with its chilling and benumbing destructiveness.

Remember the Waterfowl

I never pass through the Berkshire Hills of Massachusetts that I do not think of a young man who many years ago, leaving home for the first time, was making his way through those hills. The cold autumn evening was coming on. He was homesick. He was going into a new life, the uncertainties of which maybe frightened him a bit, and he was discouraged. Then against the sunset of the evening sky he noticed a lonely waterfowl making its way with steady wingbeat toward the South and its winter home. Young William Cullen Bryant addressed himself to that lonely voyager of the skies:

"Whither, 'midst falling dew,
   While glow the heavens with the last steps of day,
Far, through their rosy depths, dost thou pursue
   Thy solitary way?"

Unlike the bird, Bryant's heart was anxious, and lonely. "Where," he wondered, "did the bird secure that unfailing confidence as it made its way through the vast and illimitable spaces of the sky?" Then the lesson sank into his mind and he gives it to us in these concluding lines:

"He who, from zone to zone
    Guides through the boundless sky thy certain flight,
In the long way that I must tread alone
    Will lead my steps aright."

There is the real escape from fear. Get a deep, unshakable faith in the fact that you are not alone, but that God watches over you and cares for you and will bring you through all difficulties. Then you will have peace of mind. Confidence, not fear, will be yours.

Seven

THE TECHNIQUE OF SPIRITUAL POWER

Our generation, expert in technological power, is strangely inexpert in spiritual power. Adept in dealing with the natural sciences we are for the most part novices in handling the important science of spiritual forces. We have learned to draw power out of the universe in a thousand different ways. We drew power out for communication. We drew down power to operate our great turbines and machinery and for travel in space. Having tapped this power in so many practical ways, it should convince us that other and greater power lies waiting for our benefit. Accomplishments in the field of natural power, notable as they are, indubitably are but forerunners of greater achievements yet to be realized in spiritual power.

An eminent scientist declared, "Each new item of our electrical past has opened still more fertile areas in the unknown. . . . We can never reach a limit of discovery while we work." If it is true that further power lies waiting in the atom and electro-mechanics, it underscores the possibility that there are other areas than the physical where even greater power may lie. The story of invention is a bright, even amazing, page in man's history. Those who pioneer in the discovery of spiritual power may ultimately, however, be marked as greater scientists and nobler benefactors than those who have operated in the field of materialistic science. No man can logically assume that the power utilized by the natural sciences is the only possible manifestation of power in the universe. The romance of exploring in the field of spiritual power holds the possibility of being one of the most alluring adventures of our age.

Not long ago I visited Greenfield Village, that fascinating display of early Americana which was established by Mr. Henry Ford at Dearborn, Michigan. Among the interesting exhibits in the Village is the original shop of Thomas A. Edison, in which the scientist worked at Menlo Park in his early career. It has been restored by Mr. Ford with complete fidelity to detail, even to utilizing the original equipment. The shop is arranged as it appeared on the night Mr. Edison discovered the principle of the incandescent bulb many years ago.

Sitting there, I allowed my imagination free reign. I could see the great scientist back there years ago working in that shop, inwardly excited because he was on the track of a great idea and was thrilled by it. The universe was about to yield up one of its secrets hidden jealously from the beginning of time. The scien-

tific wizard ran his hands over the universe, feeling for
something which he had not yet found but instinctively
knew was almost within his reach. Finally, his restless,
searching hands stopped; he pressed; and light sprang
out of darkness. The incandescent bulb was a fact.
Night was turned into day. Candle light and gas light
faded and a new era of illumination was born.

Power for Every Need

As I lived this over in my mind, I questioned, "If
it is possible for a man to reach out into the universe
and draw down power to light our cities and homes,
why can we not reach into the same universe and
draw out spiritual power to illuminate this world, to
drive away the dark shadows of fear, prejudice, war
and economic troubles? Is there not resident in the universe another light that will shine into the darkened
corners of a man's mind and illuminate his thinking?"
We cannot agree to the assumption that the Creator
made a power to light up a room and failed to make a
power to light up a human being. To discover this
kind of power demands no scientific genius, like Edison, but simple, honorable, spiritually committed men
willing to pay the cost.

Our generation desperately needs this form of
power. We have heretofore put a naïve faith in
sophisticated philosophies and clever devices but
they have generally failed us. This broken, battered,
and disillusioned world finds little strength or healing

in ideas and points of view once so brightly, even
jauntily, cherished. Thoughtful men are realizing
that we have lost contact with the genuine sources
of power and that a generation which felt itself to be
in all ways adequate to its own needs is all but futile
in the face of overwhelming difficulties. We must
once again tap that ancient and mystic power which
in times past has saved men and nations. Our age
must discover the impotency of many of its philosophies, complacent schemes, and machineries and turn
again to that deeper force we call the power of God.

What society needs, the individual man also requires. The problem of living with oneself is for most
people the really difficult fact of life. The famous
preacher Dwight L. Moody was once asked to name
the man who had caused him more trouble than any
other man he had ever met. Unhesitatingly and quickly he replied, "The man's name is Dwight L. Moody."
I can say the same about Norman Vincent Peale. In
fact, he gets on my nerves, for he is all too ready to do
the things I do not want him to do, and he easily
fails to do the things I do want him to do. Every
honest man will make the same admission about himself.

A chief need of every individual is to find a power
or force by which he can control himself and handle
effectively the problems and burdens life lays upon
him. To realize that there is available for him a spiritual power which will carry his life forward in a
manner as different as the 747 Jet airplane from the

ox-cart should motivate him to the point of seizing the romance of spiritual power. The problem for society and the individual is to learn how to secure and use this power.

The Church a Power Center

Here is where the Church should enter the picture. Many people have a faulty conception of the Church as a dull, often lifeless, institution—and let's face it, sometimes it is. But that does not represent the truly vital Church—one that is in contact with God.

Some time ago I drove through Schenectady, New York, and passed the General Electric plant, where they generate and deal in power. I chanced to see not far away an old church which had apparently fallen into some disuse. It had a look of resigned hopelessness and defeatism about it. It occurred to me then that essentially the function of the Church is that of the General Electric Company—to release power; but the former was content, it seemed, to mumble prayers and recite creeds and perhaps live in the past. It had forgotten its purpose, which is to release for the individual and society the spiritual power inherent in the world and freely offered to those who want it and will take it.

It did that in its early days. Christianity then obviously possessed tremendous power. It became an overwhelming sensation in every community into which it came. In tragically few places is it a sensation today. Too often it seems to be old, dead stuff, which makes little or no impression on the community life. The power within Christianity, however, is not dead. It is merely impeded in its flow by hollow forms and empty formalists, and by reducing it solely to a political arm for social change. But like rivers when the spring freshets come, again and again in human history it has broken its dams and overflowed with refreshing spiritual vitality into the life of the world.

That flood, I believe, is again on the way. Religious leaders are learning that as the Church recognizes its function, teaching the simple and practical technique of spiritual power to today's men and women, it is opening the way for a new chapter in the power of the spirit. Dr. C. G. Jung, the noted psychologist, pointed out that today in ever-increasing numbers harassed people turned to the physician rather than to the minister for mental and spiritual relief and healing. In the wholly worthwhile attempt to create a new social order the Church has neglected the human beings who make up that same social order and who have been hard put to it to get a handout of spiritual bread by which to live with some degree of strength and courage in the social order that is.

Real Christianity is that to which baffled, frustrated people should be able to turn as thirsty men to a deep, cool spring where invigorating waters flow. Our fathers knew the art of spiritual power. They harnessed it to their lives and their society. One of the supreme

needs of this generation is a concrete, simple, workable
technique of spiritual principles. People must not only
be told they should pray but also be taught how to
pray; not only that they should have faith but how
to have faith. If they are told that God will help them,
they must also know in a practical sense just how to
receive that aid. In a word, we need to relearn the
definite procedure for releasing spiritual vitality in the
individual and in society. How is it to be done?

Really Get Motivated

Let us say, first of all, that formal belief in religion
or mere observance of its forms yields little practical
aid, but that personal commitment taps overflowing
reservoirs of spiritual power. A glance at the history
of religion and its effect on men illustrates this assertion. Christ, as He neared the end of His career on
earth, was on a hilltop with His disciples. In His
years of association He had become well acquainted
with these men, realizing their weakness and knowing
their strength. They were simple Galilean peasants,
ordinary run-of-the-mill fellows. Some were fisher-
men, one a tax-gatherer, and none of them had any
particular claim to distinction. Looking at them, the
Master said an apparently impossible thing: "Ye shall
receive power after the Holy Spirit has come upon
you." In current speech that was to say, "You men
are to be endowed with amazing power, the like of

which you never dreamed, when God's abiding Spirit is received into your hearts."

They were simple enough to believe that He knew what He was talking about. They were naïve enough to take Him at His word, and with what a result! The Bible, with simple eloquence, tells us that they went out and turned the world upside down, and so they did. They changed the stream of history; they inspired the rewriting of the philosophies of the world; they upset the political map for generations; they toppled autocrats off the thrones of great empires; they destroyed those empires; they established democracy; they have kept the world in ferment until now and will continue to do so until the Kingdom comes.

Fabulous Takeover

They moved forward with a power that was irresistible—these simple men. Read the story of their conquest of Athens, the intellectual capital of the ancient world. These men had no learning, but they moved up against Athens, where they encountered the great, towering intellects and a cultural life, sophisticated and haughty. These thinkers of Athens examined with speculative curiosity and intellectual dilettantism every new idea, but nothing had ever "grabbed them" or laid hold of their wills or changed their lives until these spirit-infused men came with an intellectual and spiritual force that cut through to the very heart of their skepticism. These plain peasants marched up to the Acropolis and in one of the most amazing romances of history captured in the name of Christ the intellectual citadel of their age.

How is it to be explained? On one basis only—they had tapped the secret of a power that nothing could stop. They were never more than a small fraction of the great population of the East or Europe. They were from the lower stratum of society. They had no money, no education, no social standing, no prestige—in short, no reason at all for their amazing accomplishments except the supreme one, that they had discovered the technique of an all-conquering power.

So has gone the amazing story of spiritual level throughout all history. When the moral and spiritual life of the world had fallen to a low ebb, when society had become corrupt and the Church was innocuous, there lived in the beautiful city of Assisi, down among the Umbrian Hills, a gay youth by the name of Francis. He lived for pleasure and was crowned by his companions King of the Revels. But he was not satisfied with his life, and one day in a wayside shrine he stopped for rest, little realizing the wonder about to take place. He came as most people come to the church, not expecting anything to happen. The priest was idly and indifferently reading the words of the Scriptures when the miracle happened—or was it a miracle?

Man On Fire

The cold print often thought to be lifeless began to glow. It became incandescent and fire leaped from it into the heart of Francis and he was transformed. He moved out into the roadways of Italy and into the streets of crowded cities, preaching with such winsome beauty and effectiveness that he actually transformed his age, and the fragrance of his life lingers to this very day. What had happened? He too had discovered the secret found by the disciples twelve centuries before and had become the awestruck possessor of mighty spiritual power.

Again, in the eighteenth century the saddest days in her history had fallen upon England. It was the period of Walpole, in which English morals and religion were all but prostrate. Multitudes were living in degradation and poverty. Society for the most part was licentious and rotten; politics was corrupt. Even the clergy were, some of them, men of unworthy life, and the churches, half-heartedly supported, were without spiritual influence. Into this situation, like a current of fresh air from sunlit mountain peaks, appeared one, John Wesley, and it came about in this way:

Miracle of Personal Change

One night this young clergyman, who possessed a cold, ethical philosophy but no power other than that of a brilliant intellect and good heritage, went into a meeting in Aldersgate Street. Here, as in the case of Francis, a man was reading the Scriptures. Again the cold print grew warm; it began to glow until it became incandescent with a white heat and power leaped from the Book into the heart of Wesley, who went out and preached with such eloquence and persuasion that multitudes were changed. When the story of his era was written, Green, the historian of the British people, declared that more was accomplished for England under the preaching of the Wesleys than all the victories won on land or sea by the elder Pitt. What had happened? Wesley, like Francis and the disciples, had discovered in the eighteenth century the technique of spiritual power.

Christianity may often be likened to a subterranean river which for long periods is out of sight and at low ebb, during which the ground becomes parched and vegetation withers and dies; but just when it seems as if a spiritual drought is destroying the best in civilization, lo, the river bursts forth as a sparkling fountain and floods in life-giving freshness upon a parched and weary land. Fertility is restored. The arts and sciences flourish. Learning becomes rich and good works abound. Civilization again becomes creative and culture thrives. Humanity steps up into new realms of happiness and well-being.

Too long now have we been in a dry and weary wilderness. We have no power within ourselves to restore new life to humanity. Only the fountain breaking through as in former times can save us. As the

farmer in the dust bowl gazes at the sky, longing for
rain, so does our generation seek for that rainfall of
the Spirit which will bring the greenness of new life
to a burned-out world and when men are willing to
accept the power proffered by God, they can have
it.

There was good reason why Jesus urged men to become as little children. Only in that way could they
be naïve and believing enough to take what was offered them. A simple turning of men to God with an
honest sense of need and a willingness to be guided
by Him would now, as at any other time in the world's
history, release this power, for it is not dead; it is
only quiescent. It waits for release.

How to Have Spiritual Power

How can the individual have this spiritual power?
In the releasing of spiritual power the removal of
blockades to a free flow of that power is important.
This has to do with the matter of ethical and moral
obstructions. It is at this point that thoughtful men
are realizing that the trouble with our age may not
be a lack of intellectual brilliance but, rather, moral
deficiency. Alexis Carrel, in *Man, the Unknown,* has
an unforgettable passage: "Despite the immense hopes
which humanity has placed in modern civilization,
such a civilization has failed in developing men of
sufficient intelligence and audacity to guide it along
the dangerous road on which it is stumbling. Human

beings have not grown so rapidly as the institutions sprung from their brains. It is chiefly the intellectual and moral deficiencies of the political leaders, and their ignorance, which endanger modern nations."

For some strange reason written into the constitution of the universe the power of God in spiritual form is blocked by the evil in men's lives. To the degree to which men generally seek and receive forgiveness and live a cleansed moral life does spiritual power operate in their affairs. When men are crooked, their affairs will be crooked, for obviously they cannot see straight. "As a man thinketh in his heart, so is he," is a truism for society as well as for the individual.

One night in New York City all lights north of Fifty-ninth Street suddenly flickered out. Elevators stopped running. Machines ceased to move. Movie houses became dark. Electric power was flowing all about the city ready to be used and, in fact, had been freely used, but now it was dark. Investigation revealed that in an important power station which served all of that section of the metropolis a very small foreign object had lodged at a vital contact point and had effectively shut off the electrical power of the entire universe from a section of the greatest city in the world.

Clean the Power Contact Points

Dirt has gotten in, it seems, at the contact point between human society and the power of the Eternal.

Dirt in men's minds has cut off that benign influence that could do away with wars, create an improved economic order, and bestow happiness and peace upon people everywhere. This dirt must be removed, and that cannot be done by any political party or world conference, however lofty its idealism, but only by the inflowing of fresh, cleansing tides of new moral vitality from the clean places of God.

Within man's inner life lies the secret of his outer well-being. It is this fact which makes a reinvigorated and revitalized Christianity of such urgent importance to our time. Those who regard religion as formality in worship or pious theory have assigned to it a place far too inadequate, for it has become in reality the desperately needed cohesive and curative force in life and is as vital to man's corporate and personal health as the violet rays of the sun falling upon the earth.

I once crossed the ocean on the westward voyage on the liner *Aquitania*. With me was a friend who discovered that the ship carried a ship-to-shore telephone, a novelty in those days. It was late at night when we entered the little telephone office and my friend inquired if he could talk with a friend in New Castle, Pennsylvania. Informed that he could do so, he gave the number, and placed the call. We were then a thousand miles at sea and I knew that New Castle lay five hundred miles inland. In a moment, however, my friend lifted the receiver of an ordinary telephone and conversed with complete clarity over fifteen hundred miles of water and mountains.

It so happened that at that very moment my mother was on a ship in the Pacific Ocean, off Yokohama, on the other side of the world. It occurred to me that it would be a wonderful thrill for my mother and me if I were to telephone her—from my ship in the Atlantic Ocean to hers in the Pacific. Accordingly, I inquired of the operator if I could make the call. He said that it could be done, but that the call was, of course, dependent upon my mother's ship having a telephone. I told him that it was the *President Coolidge*. He looked it up in the telephone directory and informed me that the *President Coolidge* had no telephone.

"What," I said, "is it possible that any well-regulated ship in this enlightened age should not have a telephone?" Sensing my disappointment, the operator said that even if the *President Coolidge* had a telephone, it would be very difficult to establish clear communication with my mother for the reason that whereas we were in nighttime, she was in daylight. He said it was possible to speak with comparative ease from light to light or from dark to dark—or within the same medium —but that when an attempt was made to telephone from either dark to light or from light to dark, the results were seldom satisfactory. Thus it appeared that if I wished to establish a clear communication with my mother, it would be necessary for me to go from out the dark and into the light.

So in this world of storm and struggle, sensing as we do our personal need of power and the desperate need of our fellow men everywhere, we reach out into the universe for help from One who alone can save us, but we cannot hear nor do we receive the strength we need. The fault is not with God but with ourselves. The trouble is that we are in the dark and our world is dark and our hearts are dark. When we leave that darkness, however, and move forward into the light, radiant energy comes upon us and we are endowed with power and to spare which will easily satisfy personal needs and those of society at large.

Trust God for the Power

Spiritual power is released also by faith in and surrender to God. These two terms are closely related. Because they are religious terms and therefore perhaps not clear to the average man they need interpretation. By faith we do not mean intellectual assent to a prescribed doctrine or creed. Rather do we refer to a simple trust in and dependence upon God in a manner similar to the attitude a child would have toward a loving father.

Surrender is predicated on faith but perhaps goes a step further. It has a double meaning. First, to surrender is to take something out of your life, to give it up, to part with it. Obviously, it means to give up sin of any kind or degree, gross sins of the flesh manifestly, but also the more subtle sins of the disposition. Many so-called Christians might not inappropriately be termed "segment Christians," which is to say that they have been changed or converted only in certain segments of their personalities. They may have given nine tenths of their lives to God's direction but one tenth may still belong to a lower order. Perhaps a certain clergyman may fall under this classification. When asked how his church was doing, he glumly replied, "Not so well," and then hastened to add, "but the Baptists aren't doing any better." The fact that he said it at all, to say nothing of the satisfaction implied, would indicate that at least a segment of his life needed to be surrendered.

Secondly, surrender means to put something into your life, and the thing to put in is faith, the kind of faith by which you can truly rest on God. Astonishing power is available to the person who learns to trust God completely, that is, to completely rest his life with all of its problems and burdens on God. Unfortunately, many of us do not have faith of this variety. We mumble a few creeds, live more or less respectable lives, and think we are people of faith, which we are not. Real faith is inevitably associated with lives of power and effectiveness.

I Learn to Float

I used to spend my summers on Long Island on the shores of Peconic Bay. There I enjoyed swimming, going in frequently twice a day. No one will ever

read about my swimming in the sport pages of the
daily paper, nor will I ever win any medals as a
swimmer, but I am the best floater on Long Island.
How did I learn to float? I saw people floating, and
it looked a bit easier than swimming. At any rate, I
felt a swimmer should know how to float. I inquired
of a good floater as to how it was done. His advice
was good and was to the effect that one must allow
the water to hold him up. In other words, one must
believe in the water.

Accordingly, I waded in, all the time repeating my
creed to the water: "I believe in thee, O Water. I
believe thou wilt hold me up." But I did not mean
it in my mind any more than many church attenders
mean the creeds they recite on Sunday. Nor did my
creed to the water give me any better results, for I
lay back on the water, holding myself stiff and un-
relaxed in a tense and fearful attitude. Looking up I
saw the blue sky, but only for a moment, for quickly
it turned to green and I swallowed a liberal portion of
Peconic Bay.

Clearly something was wrong with my technique
of floating. I persevered, however, and one day I lay
back upon the water completely relaxed, giving myself
to the water, without stress or tension and wholly un-
reserved. To my amazement and great satisfaction I
discovered I was floating. Beneath me was a mighty
bosom of water holding me up and sustaining me with
ease. I became conscious of a power under me that

was vast and illimitable. Such in essence is the experience people have who learn to trust God, who surrender their lives into His keeping. You hear them with happy voices saying, "Underneath are the everlasting arms," and, again, "I can do all things through Christ." Of course they can, with power like that.

Eight

HOW TO LIVE
IN A TIME LIKE THIS

How to live in a time like this—that is the question, and it's a real question, for this is not only a time that tests men's souls but their ability to live also. Ours is, and has been for some decades, a period of uncertainty for the average man. What the next day will bring no one knows. The sense of security known in other days and the old habit of planning with confidence is largely gone. A great problem of the hour seems to be security.

For youth, the past few years were years of peculiar discouragement, even frustration. A multitude of human problems both personal and social ranging all the way from racial troubles to war, inflation and pollution agitate the minds of men and disrupt relationships. Over the whole world, like Vesuvius over the Bay of Naples, looms the threat of further troubles yet to come. A dying man said to me recently: "For myself I do not regret to leave this world, for life is so ominously uncertain here. I only fear for my loved

ones, how they are going to live and what they shall
be called upon to endure in the years ahead." It is a
far-reaching problem which taxes all our powers and
ingenuity—how to live in a time like this.

Cultivate Patience

But there is a way, a very successful way, and the
prescription for it was written in a time similar to our
own, though long ago. This prescription is found in the
Bible, a book which enjoys timelessness and universality for many reasons, not the least of which is that it
is written out of human experience which, though
circumstances may, and indeed do, differ, is essentially
unchanging from generation to generation.

In a period of upheaval and uncertainty the Master
spoke these words: "In your patience ye shall win your
souls." This is at first sight a strange statement. It is,
for example, a little startling to be told that we must
win our souls. We have been in the habit of thinking
we possess a soul as a divine inheritance. It brings to
mind the statement of Browning that he believed in
the immortality of the soul—"Where a soul can be dis-
cerned." We are accustomed to think of our souls as
the fully developed gift of God. The Master meant
that the soul is, rather, like a bulb which contains
the possibility of the full-grown lily. The soul is given
to one in incipient form, and it may grow or die. "In
your patience"—you shall finally win a soul. What is
the meaning of that great word?

Set the word "patience" off by itself as an airplane might write it in letters of smoke against the sky. Look at the values that flash from it like jewels—perseverance, calmness, forbearance, philosophical composure, poise, faith. We are told that in such virtues we shall come into possession of our souls or, in other words, achieve an understanding and philosophy of our own personalities in their relation to this difficult world. Despite the noisy, clamorous, battered, disillusioned age in which we live, in the deep patience of our hearts our souls will grow until in a profound sense we have learned to overcome the world.

Now, let us take this word "patience" and, adopting it as our attitude toward life, consider how by its use we may live happily and well in a time like this. It teaches us, first of all, to live a day at a time. *Carpe diem*—seize today—is a bit of good advice, come down from pagan days. The Buddhists likewise exhort their adherents to make the most of every moment. Guatama taught that the passing beauty of a thing in nature, a gracious friendship, a noble thought, or a fleeting inspiration—all must be highly prized. Live this one day to the full without borrowing trouble about the future, is an emphatic teaching of Christianity. "Do not be troubled about tomorrow. Tomorrow will take care of itself." An old Christian hymn sings, "Lord, for tomorrow and its needs I do not pray." And a still greater hymn wisely declares,

> "I do not ask to see the distant scene;
>   One step enough for me."

Take a Step at a Time

Taking a step at a time is the best means of progress. At my summer home the garage is perhaps two hundred yards from the house and at night it is pitch dark when the lights of the car are extinguished and the garage doors are shut. I carry a flashlight to guide me along the road to the house. I have discovered that the most effective way of using my flashlight is to throw its illumination upon the path immediately ahead of me. If I lift it and throw it far ahead, its beam is soon dissipated in the darkness and I find myself falling and stumbling. When I am content to light up merely the next step or two, I keep on the path and come quickly and safely to the house.

When our thought is projected days, months, and years ahead, personal power is dissipated, and we stumble and go without direction through life. Put the force of your thought on the day at hand and let tomorrow and, indeed, all the tomorrows take care of themselves. The chances are if this day's work is done just as well as you can do it, that subsequent days will by a natural law of adjustment care for themselves. At any rate, it adds an unnecessary and unwise burden to take the tomorrows on your shoulders today.

My First Sermon

I recall my first Sunday as minister of my first church. That initial sermon lasted about twelve minutes, a fact which would doubtless cause my present congregation to sigh for the old days, which come not back. I could think of absolutely nothing more to say, and I had worked two weeks on that sermon. On the way home from church I thought, "How in the world will I prepare two sermons next Sunday?" And then in a terrifying flash came a vision of all the sermons I would have to preach until I died.

"What," I worried, "would I do about sermons twenty years hence?" These thoughts filled me with fear. Then it occurred to me that such long-projected anxieties were very foolish. Accordingly, I decided to do the next sermon as best I could and trust that those of twenty years later would take care of themselves, or, at least, I resolved not to worry about them until I came to them. I would patiently do the next one and the next in turn. This decision gave me great peace of mind.

The problem is the same whatever your occupation may be. You will do your best work and be happier if you resolutely put worries and fears of the future out of your mind and live and sincerely labor on today's task. If you do your work honestly and creatively and are living well this day, the chances are that the days to come will indeed take care of themselves. Live a day at a time is sound wisdom.

Sir William Osler, who gave much wise counsel to mankind, advised us to adopt the principle of watertight sections such as is used in constructing ocean liners—to learn to control the machinery of our lives so as to live in what he calls "day-tight" compartments.

This, he says, is the most certain way to insure safety on the voyage. "Get on the bridge," this sage doctor advised, "as captain of your life and see that, at least, the great bulkheads are in working order. Touch a button and hear at every level of your life the iron doors shutting out the past, the dead yesterdays. Touch another and shut off by a mental current the future, the unborn tomorrows. Then you are safe, safe for today."

George Herbert's advice, also, is good. "Undress your soul at night," he says, "not by self-examination but by shedding, as you do your garments, the daily sins, whether of omission or commission, and you will wake a free man with a new life." It is this kind of patience with life, this being willing to take the day as it comes and the genuine effort to do the best you can with it and, what is extremely important, the ability when it is finished to put it away without regrets and take up a new day, that will truly help one to win and possess his soul. Such is necessary to successful living in a time like this.

Keep Inner Quietness

Patience means another thing and that is inner quietness. The patient man is surely one who is unhurried in his mind and who finds it possible to relax

within. It is supremely essential that in the midst of
the confusion of this time there should be no confusion inside a man. It is at this point particularly that
Christians are effective, for from the self-contained
and poised spirit of Jesus they have discovered for
themselves what the old mystics called peace at the
center.

One thing is sure, so long as the din and jar of life
do not get into the inner essence of a man, he is safe.
So long as he can keep an inward stillness and poise,
it does not really matter what confusion reigns without. When for any cause that inner quietness gives
way and the clamor and litter of the world come
pouring into his mind, he either goes to pieces and
sinks or—God help him!—becomes cynical and hard.
Thus is seen the importance of careful attention to
the inner spiritual life, for that is a man's last citadel.

A ship in a storm at sea may be pounded hard by
the wind and waves, but if she has a steady captain
and a dry engine-room with her motors throbbing on,
she will ride out the storm. By the same token the
man who maintains peace at the center, who preserves
a place within where all the disturbing, turbulent
factors of life may be assembled and in a spirit of
detachment evaluated, will stand unbroken amidst
all tumult. It is well for the individual to learn the
art of spiritual relaxation and practice it with regularity.

A good friend, an exceedingly busy physician and
surgeon, Dr. William Seaman Bainbridge, taught me
how to live in a time like this. He carried on a pro-

digious amount of work but was always calm and filled
with the joy of living. He did enough to break down
three ordinary men. One day I went to his office to
see him about a matter of mutual concern with no
thought of my own physical condition, which was, so
far as I could see and feel, satisfactory. His waiting
room was filled with patients. The nurse told me that
he had performed two operations that morning but
that he would soon be in and without any interlude
must take up his list of waiting patients.

Accordingly, she ushered me into his private office,
where, she said, I might see him for just a moment
when he came in. Presently, as was his habit, he ar-
rived in a great rush. He dropped into a chair and I
noticed that he let his body become limp; his head
went back on the back of the chair, his legs out in
front of him; and his arms hung limply over the side
of the chair. Every muscle was relaxed. He began to
talk not about the business at hand but mentioned a
play he had recently seen and then discussed a new
book he was reading.

Then suddenly he looked at me searchingly and said,
"What's the matter with you?" The way he said it
made my face go white. "Why," I replied, breath-
lessly, "I do not know. Is anything wrong with me?"
"Why, of course," he said, "just look at you. There
you sit. You are in a hurry. You think you have so
much to do. You sit there actually gripping the arms
of your chair. Let yourself go, relax," he commanded,
"drop your head back; let your legs and arms be limp.

Now forget what you have to do. Tell me what you have been reading."

In about five minutes he snapped up in his chair, briskly took the business in hand, and in a moment or two genially ushered me out and started with fresh energy down a long line of patients. I went down the street chuckling to myself over the discovery of what subsequently proved to be one of the most important secrets of peace in the midst of life's stress and strain that I had ever found. My friend, the doctor was in a deep sense possessing his soul, his body, and his mind by the quality of patience. That is an essential element in learning to live in a time like this.

In a beautiful passage in the Bible we are taught to rise up with wings as eagles so that we may walk life's dusty way without fainting. It teaches the art of living in two worlds at the same time—the world without and the world within—but cautions us that if the world without is permitted to encroach upon the world within, trouble will result. They must work in perfect co-ordination, not overlapping nor infringing in any way, the one upon the other.

Living in a Day of Revolution

This idea of patience, quietness, and inner confidence is vitally important if one is not to be swept off his feet and suffer his equilibrium to be disturbed, if not destroyed, by this confused and tangled time. How shall we live in this age of revolution? Christianity teaches us, first of all, to keep thinking, praying and working for humanity. And Christianity has the philosophical detachment of age and experience. It has lived through many upheavals in history. It knows that the world is not going to pieces in a minute, nor, for that matter, at all. The furor of a decade cannot disturb the equilibrium of the centuries. The Christian calmly trusts the world to God. The Christian philosopher is aware that an earthquake will shake down only those things which should be shaken, but that those things which have enduring foundations will survive and by that token are the only things that should survive.

Gibbon, in his *Decline and Fall of the Roman Empire,* describes those dark days when the Goths and Huns and Vandals swept down upon Rome. They fell upon the glorious temples and palaces of the Eternal City with destructive zeal. When they had finished their depredations, however, it was observed by the thoughtful that only the filigree work, the frills and superficial ornaments, had been destroyed. The great pillars and lofty arches still remained, standing forth in an even more imperial beauty because of newly demonstrated strength inherent in their simplicity. Thus, our civilization finds itself in earthquake times. The Christian philosopher with quiet poise reminds us that the eternal verities upon which our civilization is based scarcely tremble while superficial elements, many of them worthless, are destroyed and actually should go. The confusion of our era may sound like a

terrific storm, but when it is over, the great trees
will still stand.

Frequently these days I have been reminded of an
incident in my childhood during one of the happy summers spent at the ancestral home of my grandfather
and grandmother in southern Ohio. It was one of those
old-fashioned homes so familiar to many of us who grew
up in the first quarter of this century. There was a
front room known as the parlor, which was opened
up only on special occasions—such as a wedding, a
funeral, or a visit by the minister. My grandmother did
not have the benefit of electric refrigeration; she did
not need it. That parlor was so cold in the winter-
time that she kept her butter and eggs in a crock just
inside the door. It scarcely even thawed out in the
summertime.

In the center of the room was a marble-topped
table on which a great Bible rested, fastened by big
brass clasps. On a shelf under the table was one of
the old-fashioned stereoscopes which, when placed to
the eyes, would enable one to see a picture of the
destruction of Pompeii or the glories of Niagara Falls.
On the wall was a picture of the three horses' heads,
the three horses always running and never getting
anywhere.

Over in the corner was a great shell which, when
placed to the ear, caused one to hear the roar of some
remote seabeach. In another corner was the omni-
present horsehair sofa, where I used to sit at family
prayers and which I remember because of its stiff

bristles, which were exceedingly distressing to one's anatomy. No matter how many of these bristles one pulled out while engaged in morning devotions, there seemed to be a never-ending supply.

Stormy Night

The bedroom in which I slept had a great four-poster, and even in summer when I climbed into bed at night, it was into a mammoth mattress in which I sank down so deeply that only my ears protruded. One night a tremendous storm swept down upon the little village. The wind sighed and howled about the house and struck it with such force that it seemed to tremble. I pulled the covers up over my head in fright. Then, peeking out, I saw the great trees waving back and forth, driven by the wind, making eerie shadows across the windowpane.

A roar of thunder and a flash of lightning followed, in which, for a fleeting moment, the room and the scene outside were illuminated. To me it seemed that everything was breaking and I was heartbroken because I was afraid the great trees would go down. I loved those trees. Under them I played. They were my friends. Finally, however, despite the storm, as is a little boy's way, I went off to sleep.

In the morning the room was flooded with sunlight. I sprang from bed, fearful of the destruction I would behold, when, to my relief, I saw that the ground, to be sure, was covered with debris but only that of a few old broken branches. The great trees still stood. Their roots driven deep into the good earth held them throughout many tempests.

The storms about us may be violent but in the center of it all stands with serene confidence the man with the Christian philosophy of life, because God is in his heart and he knows that God is in the world. He is not panicky, because he knows that what must go should go, and there are plenty of decadent branches whose day is done, but he also knows that the abiding realities, time-tested and good, when the storm is over, will stand as sturdily as ever. The genuine values are rooted deeply and firmly in man's cumulative experience and will endure. That, I say, is one great function which Christianity performs in an age of revolution, to contribute that calm faith in the eternal balance of things, which is a deep and true philosophy by which to live in a time like this.

The suggestion that "In your patience you shall win your own soul" indicates another help for living in a time like this, and that is the expectation that out of the difficulties of this hour a better day will come to pass. It always works that way; the pearl is developed from the pain and death of the oyster; coal which warms and cheers man came out of the decay of ancient trees; and April with its new, fresh beauty is born in dark and boisterous March. Albert Schweitzer, the eminent German scholar, musician, and world-famous Christian, paid tribute to the wholesome value of pain when he said, "The age that has no great sorrow on its heart will have no great music on its lips."

One Eye Short, One Long

Robert Browning, we are told, had strange eyes, one of short vision, the other of long. By shutting the long one he could see almost microscopic objects with the short eye, while by reversing the process, he could see sights far out of range of lesser men. It was such ability to see that caused him to lay down a couplet with mighty, deep truth in it:

"And still as the day wore on the trouble grew,
Wherefrom I guessed there would be born a star."

All of which is to say that not until it gets really dark do the beautiful stars appear. Patience of the Christian variety teaches us in these dark days to look for the bright stars of hope. This is perhaps a hard lesson, but our generation will be better for it. We have been pretty soft in our attitude toward life, expecting ease and luxury without struggle. Some bright theorists may encourage us to expect that, but the fact is that nature does not work that way. Real men are made by no soft and easy process, but by labor, sorrow, and pain.

One time at a dinner I was seated next to Walter Damrosch, famed and beloved musicmaster. I asked him to name his favorite symphony. "Oh," he replied, with a laugh, "I could not say, for to me they are all beautiful." But I was not to be put off and pressed him for an answer, saying, "If you could hear but one more symphony, which would it be?" "Well," he replied, thoughtfully, "I would want to hear the adagio from Beethoven's Ninth Symphony. You will recall," Mr. Damrosch continued, "that Beethoven wrote that work after he became deaf, and it has been often noted that in these passages he evoked new harmonies of ethereal bliss and wondrous beauty.

"They were combinations of sounds never heard before and were drawn not alone from his mental remembrance of music, but—and this is the important thing—they were new sounds evidently from a higher world. It was as if his deaf ears, having been deadened to the sounds of this present world, gave him another and inward ear, open to a higher world."

We will be fortunate if we can develop that patience of spirit which will enable us to find in our difficulties a higher and therefore deeper appreciation and under standing of the meaning of life.

Nine

CHRIST'S HEALING POWER

One of our great human problems is that of sickness and suffering. The sick are everywhere. In the city of New York it is estimated that 75,000 people are ill every day. Add to this number those who are coming down with sickness, those who are in a state of poor health and not listed officially, and those who are convalescent and the total number of sick assumes amazing proportions. In addition is that vast host of people who are mentally ill. A report of the American Psychiatric Association published in connection with one of its national meetings tells us that mental diseases have increased so rapidly in kind and quantity that more than half of the nation's hospital capacity is devoted to the care of the mentally ill.

Dr. Henry C. Link pointed out that in one year the total number of patient days in all hospitals in the United States for mental cases was 173,000,000 against 123,000,000 patient days for all other diseases. "In New York State it has been authoritatively estimated," he declared, "that hereafter one in every 22 persons born in the state will go to an institution for mental illness. Such cases represent the extremes of individual failure, but we see their intermediate symptoms in the feverish pursuit of panaceas for happiness which characterizes the whole fabric of our current national life."

People Breaking Under Stress

From all of this it is obvious that people are breaking up in their minds under the stress and strain of modern life. This generation is grievously suffering from diseases of degeneration such as heart trouble, high blood pressure, and various forms of nervous difficulty. It seems that everywhere life is unsatisfactory for multitudes of people, due to sickness, the stress of nervous tension, and the tragedy of divided personalities. Who can compute the vast number of those whose lives are out of balance, the unsatisfied people; they are sick too —men and women who are unhappy down deep in their personalities because some vital part of their nature is underdeveloped—in a word, who are frustrated by life.

Consider, also the endless number of people who are everlastingly at war with themselves, who suffer from inner conflicts. These are people who cannot sleep soundly, whose food falls short of complete tastiness, and whose days are inwardly frantic because they have no peace within themselves. Truly, the sick are

everywhere. Nor have we mentioned those who are
sick from fear and worry, those two ancient enemies
of the human spirit. Ordinarily, we do not realize the
power of fear and worry, long held, to make one
physically ill, to say nothing of causing mental illness.

No man could be any more compellingly aware of
the situation I have just described than a minister
working at the heart of America's greatest city. On
the basis of my experience in being called upon to
deal with a multitude of cases of every manner and
kind I offer it as my judgment that if America needs
any one thing today, it desperately needs the cooling
balm and the healing grace of Jesus Christ.

We need to have our nerves quieted if our bodies
and minds are to be healed and if health is to char-
acterize our life today. It ought to be obvious at this
late date that our salvation as a people cannot be
achieved wholly by scientific invention or by political
and social planning, however well conceived. Fundamentally, our salvation lies where it has always reposed,
in finding peace and rest inwardly and with it that
calm and poise without which we can never be strong
and effective.

Many are finding in spiritual principles today a
power to help the sick, using this latter term in the
general sense in which I have outlined it. Jesus Christ
frequently referred to himself as a Physician and often
in the New Testament we are told—"He healed many."
Many years ago a French physician, Doctor Coué,
came to this country. I heard him speak in the city of

Boston before an audience that packed a huge audi-
torium. He came declaring that he had the power to
heal the sick. I saw the lame, the halt, and the blind
crowd hopefully about him. They even carried people
in on stretchers, who looked up with wistful longing into his face. Many of these people went away
disappointed.

The Great Healer

As I studied this scene I thought of a Great Healer
long ago to whom also came the sick and the suffering. I could see Him with a vast throng of people
surrounding Him. There He stood, tall, strong, vigor-
ous, with the electric power of mighty physical, mental,
and moral health emanating from His personality. His
voice, clear as a silver bell and vibrant with truth,
rang out over the multitude. The people listened as
in the hush of a great awe. They were in the presence
of immortal power and they knew it. Here was a Man
through whom the tides of the Infinite were flowing,
and the people were conscious of that power. The
Bible tells us that when He had finished speaking, the
crowd rushed upon Him and "sought to touch him,
and there went power out of him and healed them
all."

Is it not possible that the same healing power is
available today no less than in the long ago, to those
who completely put their lives—mind, soul, and body—
under the influence of Jesus Christ? Is He not called

with merit the Great Physician? Dr. John Maillard, a
prominent English clergyman, in his book, *Healing in
the Name of Jesus,* advances the thesis that Jesus Christ
enjoyed the power of healing not because of His
natural compassion or of healing forces within Himself,
for the Master made no personal claims when He
healed the sick. He said, "The Father in me doeth the
works." Doctor Maillard points out that Christ was
the perfect channel through which the power and love
of God flowed, and the Gospels tell us that "as many
as touched him were made whole."

If this power is still operative—and we see no reason for assuming that it is not—it would mean that
any man today who completely opens himself to the
influence of the spiritual Christ would straight away
clear a channel within himself through which this
divine power might flow. This point of view has impressive scientific support. Dr. J. A. Hadfield, the
eminent neurologist of Oxford, pointed out that the
greatest psychologists tend toward the view that the
fundamental source of power is to be regarded as
some impulse that works through us and is not of our
own making. Bergson referred to it as the élan vital.

Janet called it the mental energy. Jung spoke of the
libido, or urge, a force which surges through our lives.
These views suggest that we are intended to be not
merely receptacles but channels of energy. When we
detach ourselves from this flow of power, we become
isolated units and gradually become inwardly barren,
with the result that all manner of infirmity and disease

develop within us. We are like little stagnant pools
cut off from the main stream of a river which in time
become festering places in which no cleansing streams
make a healthful condition possible.

Now, lest I be misunderstood, may I declare that
my attitude toward this question of Christ's healing
power is based on a working unity of scientific Christianity and the science of medicine. I have no patience
with quackery in any form. I come from a family of
doctors, merchants, and clergymen, and have a profound and unshakable faith in and affection for the
practitioner of medicine.

Send for Your Minister as Well as Doctor

Most physicians, however, agree today that there is
an ever-increasing rapprochement between religion
and medicine, and some will even say, "I believe the
patient should send for his minister when he gets sick
just as he sends for his doctor."

Other physicians indicate a growing sense of unity
between the kindred arts of physical, mental, and
spiritual healing. Dr. William Brown, of Oxford and
Kings College Hospital in London, declares, "I have
become more convinced than ever that religion is the
most important thing in life and that it is essential
to mental health." Dr. J. A. Hadfield, previously
quoted, who is also of the famous Harley Street, ex-
presses the same conviction. "I am convinced," he

says, "that the Christian religion is one of the most valuable and potent influences that we possess for producing that harmony and peace of mind and that confidence of soul which are needed to bring health and power to a large proportion of nervous patients. In some cases," he continues, "I have attempted to cure nervous cases with suggestions of quietness and confidence, but without success until I have linked these suggestions onto that faith in the power of God which is the substance of the Christian's confidence and hope. Then the patient has become strong."

Lord Dawson of Penn, physician to his late Majesty the King, has in frequent utterances testified to the aid religion can render medicine in curing the mental and physical ills of society. He has expressed the opinion that in functional and organic diseases there are reactions of mind and temperament, and "we have to study not only the material disease but the complete fabric or make-up of this or that personal illness."

It is significant in this connection to read in the British *Medical Journal*, "There is not a tissue of the human body wholly removed from the influence of spirit." This chorus is joined by the voice of Dr. C. G. Jung, the eminent Swiss physician and psychologist. "I should like to call attention," said Doctor Jung, "to the fact that among all my patients over thirty-five years of age there has not been one whose problem in the last resort was not that of finding a religious outlook on life." That statement, may I interject, is worthy of the profoundest meditation. "It is safe to

say," continues Doctor Jung, "that every one of them
fell ill because he had lost that which living religion
bestows, and none of them has been really healed who
did not regain his religious outlook."

Try Spiritual Healing

Consider that carefully, you sick man or woman.
Christ has healing power, declares this great physician.
Isn't it interesting to consider that perhaps your trouble, which you may think is a deep seated physical
malady, may be traced instead to an absence of spiritual vitality in your life? I do not say that such is the
case because I am not a physician, nor do I make any
pretense at being one. I am simply saying that it is
the judgment of some of the most discriminating minds
in the field of psychology, medicine, and religion that
a spiritual lack is the basic cause of much illness. It
might be a very helpful thing for you tonight when you
take your medicine to pray at the same time. Ask
God to come into your life and give you health. That
may do you quite as much good as your pills. Some
people who do not know what is the matter with them
may find it advantageous to join with the services of
a good physician a minister trained in spiritual healing.

Dr. Henry C. Link, the distinguished New York
psychologist whom I have previously quoted, in his
book, *The Return to Religion,* tells us that in treating
people he found himself constantly reducing his pro-

fessional and scientific facts to what amounted to the simple precepts of religion. He discovered that he could not practice his profession adequately without applied Christianity, so that he returned to religion himself after having eliminated it from his life for a number of years.

Dr. John Rathbone Oliver, professor of medicine at Johns Hopkins University, declares that the greatest psychologist or healer of the mind who ever lived is Jesus of Nazareth. "Nowadays," he says, "I sometimes hear one of my psychiatric colleagues proclaiming some new truth in connection with mental illness, and somehow the new doctrine seems to have a familiar sound. When I trace this familiarity to its source, I find myself not in the latest book by Freud or Adler, but in the Gospels. Many general principles that our Lord laid down long ago have been rediscovered by scientists and proclaimed from the housetops as something new."

Guilt Made Him Sick

The manner in which medicine and religion combine to effect healing and to bring unity to disorganized personalities may be illustrated by an incident brought to my attention by a prominent New York physician. He told me that a gentleman came to see him, complaining of not feeling well, and who, in fact, seemed very greatly distressed and gave every appearance of being in a state of illness. The physician made a com-

plete examination and informed the patient that he
could find nothing definite wrong with him.

About two weeks later the man reappeared and
said, "Doctor I want you to examine me again, for I
am really at my wits' end. I feel very bad. I am nervous
and upset. I cannot eat or sleep, and," he concluded
with a gesture of futility, "I am completely miserable."
The doctor examined him again and finally, being a
very wise man and an honest one as well, said to the
patient: "There is, as far as I can see, nothing definitely wrong with you physically. Your body is not func-
tioning normally, to be sure, but I find no evidence
of organic trouble." And then he said, "You must have
something on your mind." Then searchingly and quietly
the physician added: "You must have something on
your conscience. Have you done anything that is wrong,
that you are ashamed of?" Whereupon the patient
became very angry and vehemently said: "I will not
stand for being insulted by you. I came here for medical advice, not a sermon." So saying he stomped out
of the office.

A few days later he was back and this time in a
much chastened spirit. "Doctor," he said, "I will confess
that you put your finger on the truth of it. I have done
something very wrong." The doctor asked him to tell
his story, counseling that a complete emptying of his
mind was absolutely vital to a restoration of his health.
The patient said that some years before, his father, a
very wealthy man, had died and had bequeathed to
him and to his brother equal shares of his large estate.

Shortly thereafter the brother had gone to Europe to live, leaving the management of the estate in the hands of his brother in America, whose duty it was to send him at stated intervals his share of the income.

The brother at home, having the business entirely in his own hands, decided after a long moral struggle to "chisel off" for himself a portion of that which was due his absent brother. He thought he could get away with it, for the reason that the books were under his jurisdiction; and from that point of view no one would ever know. But—and this is the subtly important thing —he couldn't "get away with it" in his own mind. The dishonesty became in every respect like a wound in the mind that would not heal because it was the center of an infection and it kept sending off poisons throughout his system.

The doctor listened to the story of his patient until he had told it all and then said, "In what bank is your account?" The doctor sent his office boy to the bank and soon he was back with a blank check, upon receiving which the physician asked, "How much can you pay your brother?" The man stated an amount and the doctor commanded, "Write the check," which the patient did with trembling hand. Then the doctor dictated a letter to the brother who had been defrauded, in which the story was told, including the incident about the confession to the doctor, and closed by saying that he was now beginning the payment of the entire sum in default, which repayments would be made at regular and stated intervals. The patient signed

it. The letter was sealed and the doctor placed it in
his patient's hand. Together they walked to the mail
chute and the doctor instructed him to drop it.

Dropping the Letter Dropped Guilt

Dropping the letter was like dropping a tremendous
burden from the man's mind, and the physician with a
smile said to him, "You feel better now, don't you?"
The man said, "I never knew what the word relief
meant before." This physician in recounting the story
to me said that the patient, when he came to him with
this guilt on his mind, was actually ill, but that to give
him medicine or handle him in any other than by a
spiritual treatment would, in his opinion, have been
malpractice. The trouble with the man was that he
had what the psychologists call "conscience distress,"
or "a sense of guilt," which affected his entire organism. In this case the physician combined the scientific
and spiritual functions, and it is one of the happiest
illustrations I know of the essential correspondence
between medicine and religion as healing agents.

As the minister of a city church, I have been driven
by practical necessity to a liaison between religion and
the science of psychology. Into our offices is ever coming a constant and growing stream of people whose
ills are obviously related to inner lack of harmony.
With many of these our ministers can deal, but some
require both spiritual and scientific treatment. A clergy-

man must rightfully be very cautious about overlapping
on the field of the physician. There was a day when the
clergyman would deal with people in trouble by simply
telling them to pray and trust God, or with the sinful
by admonishing them to confess their sins and be converted. This still remains the fundamental method of
healing, but the technique by which this eternally
modern treatment is to be applied has advanced in
skill over that used by our fathers.

We Form a Clinic

My deficiencies in scientific healing technique led
me to cast around for a method by which the Church
might more adequately deal with the increasing number of personal problems presented. I established a
working partnership with a great psychiatrist, Dr.
Smiley Blanton, who was interested in combining the
therapy of psychiatry with that of the pastor. Dr.
Blanton firmly believed that while psychological medicine had its own field and discipline, it had a natural
relationship with the discipline of pastoral therapy.

We began seeing troubled people separately, then
would consult as to the best procedures to employ.
The results were so phenomenal as to encourage us
to bring other ministers, psychologists and psychiatrists
into the working relationship.

Now after thirty years we are formed into the American Foundation of Religion and Psychiatry at 3 West
29th Street, New York City.

Some authorities competent to pass judgment have declared this organization to represent one of the greatest advances in pastoral work in our time. Bringing together as it does the therapy of religion with that of psychological medicine, it has brought healing to many. This clinic is open to everyone who desires its services.

Christ's Healing Power a Fact

Christ's healing power is not presented in this book as a theory but as a demonstrated fact. I have personally seen the workings of spiritual forces in cases of nervous trouble and indeed in various types of illness; so effective have they been that there remains in my mind a profound conviction that the future will witness remarkable advance in the therapeutic usage of religion. Dealing with people day-by-day, I have become convinced that in spiritual power we possess a valuable healing agent and I have been continually impressed by the way in which our "medicine" works. It has been demonstrated that if an individual will learn to believe and completely surrender himself to God, he will open himself to the inflowing of the healing grace of God.

Alexis Carrel in *Man, the Unknown*, previously referred to, substantiates this point of view. Doctor Carrel offers it as his conviction that there is a much deeper relationship between psychological and even physiological processes and the spiritual life than we have supposed. Indeed, he assumes an advanced position by describing with apparent approval the recorded healings of Lourdes, and declares on the basis of those cures that "the only condition indispensable to the phenomenon (of healing) is prayer." He gives us the further interesting suggestion that "there is no need for the patient himself to pray . . . it is sufficient that someone around him be in a state of prayer."

We are not prepared to evaluate the position of Doctor Carrel, but his undisputed scientific eminence lends significance to his contribution to this field. In all healing he regards prayer as of profound importance but warns, and wisely, that "prayer should be understood not as a mere mechanical recitation of formulas but as absorption of the consciousness" in God. It means to put all thoughts of self out of the mind, to discard every vestige of will, to put oneself completely under the will of God or, to use Carrel's definition, "Prayer is man offering himself to God." It is man standing before God as the canvas stands before the painter. The canvas in effect says to the painter, "I am empty; fill me as you will," and the artist fills the canvas full of his own genius. Taking this attitude toward the power of God, any sufferer is likely to find an access of new strength and healing.

Three Healing Stories

Three incidents from my personal experience serve to illustrate the practical outworking of this principle.

Three people well known to me who actually surrendered themselves to God by an act of childlike
faith received new life in a manner so astoundingly
conclusive as to leave no room for doubt that there
is in applied Christianity a profound healing power
available for all men everywhere.

The first is my own mother, who began ₊to break
physically under strain and tension. She consulted a
noted heart specialist, who after an examination asked
her the unexpected question, "Madam, are you a Christian?" To which she in surprise replied, "Why, yes, I
consider myself a Christian." She recited to him the
several and important positions in which she was
rendering Christian service. He listened and shook his
head. "No, madam, despite all of that I doubt if you
are a real Christian." He explained his statement by
saying, "I understand that being a Christian means to
have childlike faith and trust, to believe that God loves
you and exercises watchful care over you, to believe
that you can talk to Him and by prayer and by faith
receive from Him strength sufficient to offset the strain
of life. In this sort of Christianity you, like most of
us," he added, "are deficient. You believe all these
things; now go out and practice them and I believe
you will get well. So," he concluded, "here is my
prescription. Go off to a quiet place alone and think
about God and get His peace into your mind, spirit
and body."

She took his surprising advice and went out on Cape
Ann, a rocky promontory on the Massachusetts coast.

There each day she sat by the sea until she truly knew that "deep calleth unto deep." She listened to the long roar of the waters as they surged against the rocks. The clean, vagrant winds swept the cobwebs from her mind. She beheld the wide sweep of the dark blue ocean and it came over her that there is unmistakably "a wideness in God's mercy like the wideness of the sea." At first her eyes wearily rested on the near-by rocks and waves, but gradually she lifted them to the far horizon until presently the vastness of the tumbling sea brought home to her that vastness which is God. After many days of this He who long ago spoke the word of peace on Galilee spoke peace to her too. The marvelous recuperative power of God manifested itself in her so that her body and spirit took on a new vigor and vitality that literally amounted to a re-creation.

The second person who experienced the restoration of surrendered faith is a distinguished public official. His life was despaired of and he had been given to understand he must cease work and carefully guard himself if he was even to live. On the morning after this blow was dealt him he said he awakened to see the sunlight streaming into his room. Lying in bed he thought of Christ and how long ago the Master helped and healed people. He closed his eyes and as simply as a child prayed something like this: "Lord, You know what they told me yesterday. I do not want to quit, for I have important work to do for Thee. I am going to get up and go to work and put myself in Your hands. If You want me to go on, You will allow me to continue. If You feel my work is ended, You will take me home to Yourself. Whatever You want for me will be all right with me."

He says that he felt a great peace after praying in this way. He arose and did a hard day's work. The next morning before arising he prayed again: "Lord, we had a great day together yesterday. Now another day is here. You are with me, and I will have no fear. If You want me to work this day, Lord, I shall be glad. I am in Your hands." So day after day he has prayed through the years. He literally lives with Christ as a Companion. Proceeding in that way, he has opened his life to new peace and strength, thus aiding nature to rebuild his health. Watching him doing his prodigious work, involving important decisions and policies, the strain of which would break down stronger men, one is aware, from the deep peace on his face and in his eyes, that he has found a tremendous healing secret.

Late one night a physician telephoned and asked me to come to an address where he had a patient suffering from nervous and physical breakdown. The doctor said, "I think this man needs some of your kind of medicine." Presently I stood by the door of the house, but before pressing the bell I bowed my head in the darkness in a moment of prayer, reminding God that I had no power or wisdom and asking Him to guide me in what I should do and say. The doctor led me into the room saying, "Our patient needs a deep peace and a power beyond himself to which he may cling for the strength which he does not have in himself."

I will confess I scarcely knew what to do, but I did not need to know, for when one wants with all his heart to have God's help, he gets it, and I found myself quoting various passages of Scripture such as— "The Lord is my shepherd; I shall not want. He maketh me to lie down in green pastures: he leadeth me beside the still waters. He restoreth my soul." Other Scripture passages came to mind and I quoted them in full.

Here an almost uncanny thing occurred. Some of these passages I did not know by heart and afterward when I attempted to recite them from memory I failed. Of course, many readings of them had given me a certain familiarity with them but the experience lent new meaning to the verse: "Take no thought beforehand what ye shall speak, . . . but whatsoever shall be given you in that hour, that speak ye: for it is not ye that speak, but the Holy Ghost." Indeed I felt myself to be but a mouthpiece for Someone of whose healing power I was the awestruck witness.

Presently the patient turned to me, with his haunting, desperate eyes seeming to search my mind. I never had anybody look into my inmost mind as he did. He looked me through and through for any sign of uncertainty as he said, "Can Jesus Christ do anything for a man like me, or is it all just religious talk and bunk?" I replied, "If you trust Him like a little child, relaxing and resting upon Him, He will give peace and healing."

He still looked at me searchingly, then said simply and in a very moving manner, "Help me, Christ." He continued that trust in God, and he had a wise and skillful medical man who helped him. That was years ago. Today he is the efficient head of an important educational institution, and when I watched him directing a large meeting some time ago, he saw me studying him and smiled across the room at me. As I bade him good-by later he said: "Don't worry about me ever again. I know where my strength lies."

Ask a man like that if there is healing power in religious faith. He knows. So may you and I. It is so simple and yet so wonderful. The secret is in sincere faith and surrender of will, to put your life with all of its problems in God's hands. That will give a superb all rightness to your life, endowing you with that calm philosophy by which you will know truly that "all things work together for good to those who love God."

Ten

"WHY NOT TRY GOD?"

Some years ago a motion-picture actress took to preaching. Mary Pickford wrote a little book entitled *Why Not Try God?* which rated for a considerable period as a best seller. This chapter is in no way a review of that book. I have merely appropriated its title and am glad to acknowledge a debt of inspiration.

In her book the author describes a tremendous secret, but it is not a new secret. In fact, it is very old. It is new only to him who finds it for the first time. The writer of the book of Psalms found it long ago. "My expectation," he declared, "is from him," which is to say with childlike faith that he expected God to do for him what needed to be done. Why not try God? Why not, indeed?

You who have a great burden upon your heart, you have tried many other devices for relief. You have sought elsewhere for heartease. Why not try God? You who are worried and anxious, why not try God? You who are morally weak, you have mistakenly looked

169

into yourself for strength and found it not, why not try God? You who have sorrow and are acquainted with grief, upon whom rests the heavy weight of affliction, you find little help in the world to take that ache out of your heart—why not try God? Here is a fabulous fact. Whatsoever your problem, it can be solved; whatsoever your burden, it can be lightened; whatsoever your sorrow, it can be assuaged; whatsoever your anxiety, it can be relieved; whatsoever your sin, it can be cleansed and forgiven.

Doubtless most of us have prayed to God more or less earnestly. We have made feeble and sporadic attempts to take hold of divine resources, but our efforts may have been largely futile. The real question is—Have we ever wholeheartedly, sincerely, and insistently tried God? Nearly everybody believes in God, to some degree at least. The number of one hundred per cent, thorough-going atheists has always been small. Not a few who are philosophical atheists in the daytime become practical theists at night when darkness falls. We believe God can do all things. We have seen evidences of it in many lives. We know that some have tried Him and found it worth while, but have we ever actually tried Him for ourselves?

Many of us are like Doctor Manette, about whom Dickens weaves a wistful story in his novel, *A Tale of Two Cities*. The Doctor had been in prison for twenty years prior to the French Revolution, which freed him. In prison he learned the trade of a cobbler and in the gloom of a cell spent his days tapping shoes. Finally the day came when he was offered his liberty and let out into the sunlight, but freedom terrified him. He had been too long in the shadows of a cell and strangely enough had grown in his soul to love it.

Accordingly, a servant was given the duty of locking him at night in an attic room about the size of his old cell, and there through the latticework he could be seen in a twilight gloom, tapping out shoes. Similarly, in the narrowness and weakness of our imprisoned lives we are led to the open door of a liberty which, God help us, we are afraid to take. We are offered magnificent powers which we will not accept. God with His illimitable resources is at our personal disposal; yet we do not try Him.

Expect Great Things

The wise psalmist, however, was not so. He said, "My expectation is from him." He expected help from God and he found it. When one confidently expects God's aid, the great truth is there is no area of life where God cannot and will not tremendously help. How do I know this, you ask? Why am I so positive of it? This I know because of personal experience. God has helped me. To Him I personally owe an everlasting debt of gratitude. I called upon Him myself; I tried Him myself and found Him reliable. Besides my own personal testimony I have been impressed by the experience of others whom I have known. I have myself seen God help people in a perfectly marvelous way. There is not the least shadow of a doubt about this fact in my mind. This is not a theory, but absolute truth.

There are at least two reasons why people do not receive help from God. The first is that they really do not expect to. Their faith is weak. They pray more or less out of habit or because it is the orthodox thing to do, or because, frankly, they do not know anything else to do, but they would be the most amazed people in the world if anything actually happened as a result of their prayers. They pray but they do not really believe in it.

If, on the contrary, out of a sense of great need you ask God's help and then live on the assumption that God is helping, if the need is sincere and the faith is real, then He will help. If you are in great trouble or need God will help you if you will allow Him to. As a matter of fact, if you try God with absolute expectation, you will find it overwhelmingly practical. First of all, it will do something to your own personality to have that sort of faith; it will make it stronger, unifying and drawing to a focus the powers which in your weakness are being dissipated. It will consolidate your powers so that God can work through you to help you help yourself. Even over and above that, however, in ways that are past finding out, experience through long centuries has demonstrated the irrefutable fact that the man who lays his burdens absolutely and completely on the Lord will find that the entire universe will help him.

One of My Greatest Experiences

This fact I know to be true by the greatest of all tests—that of personal experience. Years ago I was the lone passenger in a chair car on a train traveling through central Ohio. For some time I had been under great strain, which was drawing heavily upon my nerve strength. Worries and fears were haunting me by day and disturbing my nights. To add further to my unhappiness a profound sense of failure had cast a heavy pall upon my spirit. On that train I was working on a sermon for the following Sunday upon the topic—"The Secret of Power." It suddenly occurred to me that the topic was ironical, for I certainly was not the possessor of power and so what right had I to discuss such a question?

Years before I had experienced the power of religion by conversion, which was in every sense real and valid. But the force of that experience of God in my life had become seemingly if not spent, at least reduced. I was now trying to get along on my own power, the vast force of God being neglected and unused. I ceased working on the sermon and in desperation of spirit bowed my head in prayer. I have prayed since childhood, but my experience has been like that of Lowell as portrayed in "The Cathedral":

"I, who still pray at morning and at eve,
Loving those roots that bind us to the past
And prizing more than Plato things I learned
At that best academy—a mother's knee,

Thrice in my life perhaps have truly prayed,
Thrice stirred below my conscious self
Have felt that perfect disenthrallment, which is God."

So in my prayer something wonderful happened. In
a moment of illumination, like a sudden flash of lightning on a dark night, revealing in clarity a hitherto
hidden landscape, so I saw into the secret of spiritual
power. But more importantly even than that was that
I felt under me a vast power like a full incoming tide
which lifts a stranded vessel from the shallows. It was
overwhelming and awe-inspiring. A great peace set-
tled upon my heart; a deep sense of rest came to
me; and overtopping all was a realization of the presence of God as the source of strength. There on that
train when least expected came an experience which
changed my life, a genuine discovery of God. As Bliss
Carman writes perhaps out of a similar transformation:

"Then suddenly all unaware
I heard God's voice on the air."

The reality of that experience could not be shaken
by all of the skepticism in the world. Like Abt Vogler
I say, "The rest may reason and welcome, but I know."
Let them call it unscientific if they wish or disparage
it in any way they desire; I know beyond the shadow
of a doubt that in that moment, or instant of time,
the wonder which is God touched my spirit and took
away my weakness, my fears, my sins, and gave me
strength. The secret was that my prayer for once was
one of absolute and complete surrender. Weary and

discouraged by living upon my meager power, I threw myself upon God, saying: "Anything You want to do with me, God, is all right. I give my life to You. I am in Your hands." I had said that often before and had meant it after a fashion, but the surrender now was not partial but complete. Since then the high tide of that experience has ebbed and flowed but the shallows have never reappeared. By a constant daily surrender to God I have discovered that the Divine Power is available for my life. I would not exchange this secret for anything in the world. So I say to you, "Why not try God?" It will work for you too, if you surrender yourself in complete faith.

When God Becomes Real to You

The second reason many of us do not receive help from God is because, frankly, God is not real to us, and He must be if we are to have dealings with Him. Academically we accept theories about God, but they remain for us only theories no matter what vital personal experience others may describe. What can one do that he may himself experience the reality of God in dealing with his problems?

If we made our relationship to God simpler, less philosophical and theological, it would be more effective and meaningful. The value of the childlike attitude of man to God cannot be overstressed. For most of us the idea of God is a great abstraction and a philosophical idea, thin-blooded and lacking in vitality. Making God real is a problem with which the greatest minds have struggled. Ages ago Plato expressed a deep desire that the moral law might become a living personality of flesh and blood so that men could become intimately acquainted with its beauty and power.

George Eliot likewise expressed the thought that great ideas dazzle us without actually taking hold of our minds, but when they appear in a personality, we love them and take them to our hearts. Thus it is evident that we need to acquire a spiritual technique by which we can personalize God in such a way that His reality becomes definite. This has been splendidly illustrated by Leslie D. Weatherhead, who tells of an old Scotsman who was very ill. His minister called to see him. The old man directed the attention of the minister to the fact that near his bed was a vacant chair and explained its presence by saying that in his early years he had found it difficult to pray, often falling asleep on his knees because he was so tired after his day's labor.

He said that even if he kept awake, it was often with the greatest difficulty that he kept his thoughts from wandering. He became worried about it and spoke to his minister, who said, "Do not think that you must kneel down to pray. Just sit down," he said, "and put a chair opposite you and imagine that Jesus is in it and talk to Him as you would to a long-time friend." The Scotsman continued, "I have been doing that ever since, and it works." A week later the daughter of the old Scot drove up to the minister's house and sobbed: "Father died in the night. I had no idea death could be so near. I had just gone to lie down for an hour or so, he seemed to be sleeping so comfortably, and when I went back, he was dead. He hadn't moved since I saw him except that his hand was out on the empty chair by the side of the bed. Isn't that strange?" "No," said the minister, "it is not so strange. I understand." The old man had a great secret. He had made God an actual factor in his daily life and living with Him in that way had found that faith was not a process of imagination, as some might declare it to be, but that God, through the years, had become increasingly a real Person to him.

God Helps a Young Man

A young man who was making a desperate struggle against an overwhelming temptation, and suffering repeated defeats, came to me. I advised him to adopt the policy of imagining that Jesus Christ in person was walking by his side and when the temptation came to ask Christ to help him overcome it. This, of course, at the start was to him only imagination, but he told me later that he soon became convinced it was more than imagination, for he clearly felt upon him a restraining hand and the force of a Personality that gave him lasting victory.

This experience has happened in the case of too many rational people to be lightly disposed of on the grounds of illusion. What scientific right has any man to say the presence of Christ is not real merely because he has not experienced it? Once in Wordsworth's garden at Grasmere I recalled that in that place he saw a great sight:

> "Hence in a season of calm weather
>   Though inland far we be,
>   Our souls have sight of that immortal sea
>   Which brought us hither,
>   Can in a moment travel thither,
>   And see the children sport upon the shore,
>   And hear the mighty waters rolling evermore."

I could not see that, but who am I to deny the validity of the vision of sharper eyes than mine.

Once on a cold day in London, Francis Thompson saw a ladder let down from heaven to Charing Cross and again one dark night he saw Christ walking, not on Gennesaret but the Thames. I never saw that, but because I may be spiritually dull must I expect Francis Thompson to be equally so? But I do not argue a philosophical speculation. I state a device for making Christ a real Person, a device which has been practiced successfully by so many sensible people that I have no doubts about it at all.

America, Try God

Why not try God? This is a most insistent question, and is fraught with more significance than any proposition we can consider today. As a matter of fact, it may be not inappropriately termed the question of the hour: "America, why not try God?" Socially, we have tried many man-conceived devices, both good and bad, with what result? We have assumed that by merely tinkering with the social machinery a forward motion might be achieved. Some people in discouragement have even thrown down their wrenches and cried loudly that the old machine should be scrapped and a new one created. The old machine is bad enough, to be sure, and surely needs repairing if not many new parts. This attitude does not take account of the fact, however, that if a new social mechanism laid down to the order of the most punctilious and exacting were built, it would not carry humanity forward without the one vital factor of power.

A machine cannot run without power. It may be that we have been erroneously giving our attention to forms when our need is power to endow lifeless forms with vitality. It ought to be obvious that no generation can lift itself for a sustained period by its own bootstraps. It is becoming increasingly evident that we cannot extricate ourselves from a social and spiritual morass by merely fumbling with materialistic processes. Our problems are too great for any one mind or any group of minds. If our minds, however, are reinforced by a greater intelligence which is lifted above the dust and confusion of the streets, we shall be endowed with power to think clearly and act wisely.

Above and beyond that, we shall be led by intuitions and insights more discerning and effective than would be allowed by the limitations of our apparent capacity. If we accept the theory that God can work in an individual life, it follows as a logical assumption that He can work in the collective life of mankind. The laws of God's working in individual lives are the laws for His operation in the life of society. If an individual man expects to receive the help of God, he must live the godlike life. Accordingly, a nation desiring the help of God must proceed in its activity on a moral, spiritual, and ethical basis.

If we, as a people, set ourselves to do what is right ethically and spiritually, our world will have a deep tendency to become right. How can we do right, however, human nature being what it is? Here is where God enters the scene. Human nature becomes more than human nature when He assumes control, and whereas before it was weak and ineffective, it now becomes strong and achieves notable attainments. As the Old Testament has it in a marvelous line—"The people that do know their God shall be strong and do exploits."

Belief in Heaven and Hell Made America

Roger Babson wrote on the title, *The New Dilemma*. In it occurs this strange statement: "Although few of you believe in heaven and in hell like your grandparents, it was this belief in heaven and hell which made this nation." Mr. Babson does not strictly mean, I assume, that a theological acceptance of the doctrine of heaven or of hell would make or break a nation. What he is saying, I take it, is that a nation succeeds or fails depending upon whether or not it possesses a clearly defined sense of right and wrong. It is a well-known fact that the sharp line of demarcation between right and wrong has been dulled in the mind of the average American in recent years. They have blended together in our thinking in such a way that many people frankly do not know where right ends and wrong begins.

Our fathers, however, had no doubt about it, as Mr. Babson indicates. Whereas in earlier years people were either on the side of right or of wrong, today most of us are in that vast border country between the two. We need to reduce the extent of this border country and sharpen up again the distinction in ethical concepts. That would be accomplished by turning again to God as a spiritual reality, for when God takes hold of a human life, the first thing to happen is a quickening of the instinctive knowledge of the difference between right and wrong. God will help America, therefore, in no magical fashion, but in the practical way of showing us what is right and giving us the power within ourselves to do right. The practical outworking of what is right would, of course, mean a new birth of a spirit of good and a wider recognition and application of the principle of human brotherhood.

We must discover that human progress is not built about great ideas, but about great personalities. Fascism, for example, was built not about the philosophy of that movement but about the personalities of Mussolini and Hitler. Communism centered not half so much about the philosophy of Karl Marx as it did about the personality of Lenin. He gave it life and made it real. So the power to transform and save our time will be not by great ideas, however magnificent they may be, but essentially by putting the spirit of the Man of Galilee at the center of our national life. Then, truly, the world will come out right. How insistent the question is and with what infinite significance it comes to us—America, why not try God?

If You Have Sorrows or Sins
Try God for Relief

You there with the burden of sorrow, why not try God? He understands sorrow. He sent Jesus here as the Master Himself said, "to heal the brokenhearted and to set at liberty them that are bruised." He was a man of sorrows and acquainted with grief and sends to all sorrowing and heavily burdened people a winsome and wonderful invitation—"Come unto me, all ye that labor and are heavy laden, and I will give you rest." Sorrow, heartache, the sense of loss, the reality of separation come to all men impartially. All of us must ultimately bear grief. From it there is no escape but for it there is a marvelous antidote. The secret is contained in the words—"My expectation is from him." So it may be, for He will not fail us. Those who have tried God sincerely have discovered a priceless secret, for He steals into their hearts in sorrow—as Bryant has it—

> "With a mild and healing sympathy
>   That steals away its sharpness
> Ere he is aware."

Why not try God, you who have a sin in your life? It is very hard to have sin and guilt on one's soul. Sin is not a fantasy. Tolstoy and Ibsen, two of the greatest masters of the human spirit, substantiated the preacher's emphasis on the reality and terror of sin. It does become, as Ibsen graphically declares, "a ghost to haunt a man." A sin in a man's life relentlessly pursues him like some hound of hell. It has ever been so. Aeschylus, generations ago, told the story of Orestes, who committed a sin and later described its pursuit of him in the picturesque phrase: "He could not escape from the furies." There can be no abiding peace or happiness in the life of any individual if there is a sin festering within him.

There is a strange something within us whereby we are hailed before a judge in our own soul who convicts us. Call this conscience, if you will, it is nevertheless a relentless, if withal, a fair judge. Every man who has done wrong and who has not been forgiven can readily understand the plaintive words of Macbeth, who, with the stain of blood upon his hands and the memory of a crime on his mind, becomes increasingly more frantic and desperate and one day turns to the court physician with this piteous question:

"Canst thou minister to a mind diseased?
Pluck from the memory a rooted sorrow,
Raze out the written troubles of the brain?
And with some sweet, oblivious antidote
Cleanse the stuffed bosom from the perilous stuff
Which weighs upon the heart?"

The physician sadly shook his head and answered, "Therein the patient must minister to himself." I am sure, however, that Shakespeare with his shrewd knowledge of men would agree that the patient cannot really minister to himself. No man is strong enough to take out of his own life the painful memory and sting of past misdeeds. There is, however, thank God, a Great Physician who can perform this healing operation. I refer to that Physician of Souls who when He places His hand upon the life of a willing patient, draws out of him with sure skill the dark poison which has infected his mind and soul and destroyed the peace and happiness of life. He has done it for many happy men and women through the years. He can do it for you.

Why not try God?

MORE . . .

ABOUT THE AUTHOR AND HIS WORK

NORMAN VINCENT PEALE is the author of 20 books, of which *The Power of Positive Thinking,* one of the most successful books ever published, has been translated into 33 languages, with a sale of more than 3,000,000 copies. The title has become part of the language of the land. A recent book, *Enthusiasm Makes The Difference,* has had wide circulation among business and sales groups, as well as individuals. Norman Vincent Peale's *Treasury of Courage and Confidence* is the author's latest book preceding this edition of *The New Art of Living.*

Dr. Peale is minister of Marble Collegiate Church, Fifth Avenue and 29th Street, New York, where he speaks to 3,000 people every Sunday.

He is president and co-founder of the American Foundation of Religion and Psychiatry.

A weekly column, "Confident Living," appears in 200 newspapers with a total readership of 25,000,000.

He is co-editor with Mrs. Peale of the inspirational monthly magazine, *Guideposts,* having a circulation of 2,000,000.

Mrs. Peale is the author of *The Adventure of Being A Wife,* published in 1971, and she is also Editor and General Secretary of the Foundation for Christian Living, Pawling, New York 12564.

In 1940, Dr. and Mrs. Peale established the non-profit Foundation for Christian Living for the purpose of publishing and sending out inspirational material, including printed sermons and booklets. By these means Dr. Peale seeks to motivate people to a deeper spiritual life and to tell how it can be accomplished through very practical and simple spiritual techniques.

Since its establishment, the Foundation has published and distributed more than 200 million pieces of literature. This work is done entirely by mail through the distribution of monthly inspirational messages (the sermons of Dr. Peale and the feature articles which he selects), helpful programs (21 booklets), formulas of action (the six Pocket Cards), and steps for accomplishment and achievement (the thirteen How Cards).

These materials are sent regularly to more than half a million people throughout the world. (There is no stated charge for the Foundation's publications; the work is entirely supported by voluntary contributions.) In addition the Foundation makes special arrangements to send, free of charge, devotional and inspirational literature to hospitals, nursing homes, prisons, the Salvation Army, youth centers and the Armed Services.

A sample packet of exciting motivational spiritual techniques is available simply by writing for:
THE NEW ART OF LIVING SAMPLE PACKET
Foundation for Christian Living
Pawling, New York   12564
You will receive Dr. Peale's booklet, YOU CAN OVERCOME ANY PROBLEM, the monthly sermons, How Card #10 entitled: "How to Have Faith," and Pocket Card #3, "The Way to Have the Power of Enthusiasm."